Dear Mrs. B

Dear Mrs. B

The Unplanned Lessons of a
Special Education Teacher

C'Anna Bergman-Hill

Book design by Joseph Gratz

This memoir is dedicated to my sons,
Jackson and Alexander,
"Teacher's Kids,"
who continue to give meaning
to all I endeavor
to do or be.

And to Kate,
who bought my first book.
I miss you.

Dear Readers,

This is a memoir of my working life as a Special Education teacher. all names of individuals, organizations, and locations have been changed or generalized.

Many thanks for sharing my career memories and my life lessons. I would love to hear from you.

Warmly,
C'Anna aka Mrs. B

cannabergmanhill @ gmail. com

I couldn't have said it better than my student John.

Introduction

I worked in Special Education for thirty-eight years. As educators we made lesson plans daily. Having a plan is important because all teachers and perhaps most especially special education teachers encounter many surprises during the school day. Having a plan keeps us focused and accountable for what we want to teach. However, the joy of teaching is to make the most of the spontaneous teaching moments that pop up frequently if you pay attention. It is that zing of "aha," that makes learning come to life, that instinct to just go with It, knowing that *it* is absolutely *right* at the moment. This is what gets students excited about learning, and what makes teaching an exhilarating career choice. These illuminating and expandable moments are like the wickedly successful backhand shot in tennis that makes up for too many botched serves and frustrating net smashes.

Many of these "aha" moments are not just about a specific academic lesson at all. They are about life itself. In time you realize that there are many lessons learned in teaching that could never be anticipated and never planned. What follows in this memoir are some of my unplanned lessons. Who indeed is the teacher and who is the student? How many moments of enlightenment and joy do we miss if we don't pay attention? And where does the education world leave off and life itself begin? My favorite poem by Elizabeth Barrett Browning gives a flavor of what I am talking about:

Earth's crammed with heaven,
And every common bush afire with God:
But only he who sees, takes off his shoes,
The rest sit around it, and pluck blackberries.

A Word About Camelot

"Camelot" was the first movie I ever saw. It was fall of 1968, and I was sixteen years old. Growing up in a Mennonite family, we did not go to movies. However this movie was recommended by my high school World Literature teacher, and education being highly valued in our home, I was given permission by my parents to attend. Vanessa Redgrave and the other actors in the splendid scenes of "Camelot" made a staggering impression on me, movie virgin. The ideas and music of "Camelot" have stayed with me to this day.

As I was writing this memoir, I found myself referring to a couple of particularly satisfying working environments as being "like Camelot." The Camelot of King Arthur legend is fictional and is located nowhere in particular, and could indeed be anywhere at all. I love that concept! In 1960, John F. Kennedy's presidency was referred to as Camelot because he was a leader with a sparkling style, representing a new vision. His short presidency was a time when a great crowd of Americans felt potential and promise for the future. Many were inspired to serve, to work, to dream and to believe in a new and rich age for all Americans and citizens across the world. Jacqueline Kennedy famously repeated the musical words, "Don't let it be forgot that once there was a spot for one brief shining moment that was known as Camelot," and then went on to lament that with her husband's death, "There would never be another Camelot again…it will never be that way again." But we were forever changed by that time.

Through my years of work in Special Education, the good work of teaching was carried out by multitudes of educators, during rough times and smooth. Nothing would ever have been accomplished if we could only do good teaching during periods of united vision like in the Camelot of my dreams. Instead, we worked through major challenges, through periods of a dulling lack of inspiration, and public assaults on the dignity of our occupation. Regardless of circumstances, teachers carried on to serve the children and families.

But there were times, places, and individuals, here and there along the way, that made my work feel like Camelot. Not the story book Camelot of King Arthur, but a nitty-gritty, inspired place where real people supported each other, learning was cherished, problems were addressed in positive ways, priorities were clear and pure, and coming to work was an absolute joy. But just like the Camelot of fiction, and sadly just like the Camelot we imagined was JFK's presidency, it can all be gone in a blink. Camelot takes great nurturing and care to survive. I am thrilled that I experienced this "place" on a few occasions in my working life because even when those rarefied times were altered or gone, *one is never the same after having experienced Camelot.*

Some Background Disclosures

College was a time when I felt invincible. My generation's opinions were righteous, capable of changing the world: full of justice and truth. That was how I experienced my four years at a small Central California private college. I spent my college days in a four-year bubble nurturing the illusion that the whole world thought I was pretty special. It was hard not to imagine that the future was at my beck and call.

Probably the truth of the matter was that I was a fairly good student in the classes I enjoyed, and I managed to avoid as many classes as possible in the areas that did not come easily to me. I had a double major, in English and Communication. Although I loved the academic world, I did not challenge myself much outside my comfort zone. Science was my brother's domain. I knew I would never enter the education field because it was so traditional. I also knew I wouldn't choose that other traditional women's occupation, a nurse because I did not see myself as sympathetic enough to care for others. In the age of counter culture, business did not interest me. I played with the idea of going into library science, having worked in the college library for four years and having spent my childhood in our local town library, but for several reasons, that career didn't work out. For the most part, I was too busy relishing college life, and indulging in my love of humanities studies, to give much thought to what would happen when I graduated. That was years away...months...then days, and finally, surprisingly suddenly, it happened. June of 1973. I was no longer a college student. I needed to work and I needed a career that would be rewarding to me. It was soon clear that I needed something. Graduate school did not appeal to me. What to do?

I did need something. I was soon in the doldrums with the only job I could find: file clerk. I spent too much time watching the clock. I was bored. Other than library work where few jobs were available at that time, I was not qualified or trained for anything as far as I could see. My lack of specific skills and training left it hard for me to see my potential. While the year after I graduated from college was a terrible time of loose ends and lack of identity, in retrospect it was a valuable gift. It woke me up, gave me perspective, and brought me down from my high horse. That miserable year gave me an honest look at myself. I had one thing going for myself—my youth! Of course there was more. I was reasonably bright, hard-working, and finally, open for the unplanned lessons of life.

I married young, right after college. A serious history student, my husband worked at the local convention center on the custodial crew. Other than a back-stage vantage point at rock concerts, and a chance to tread cautiously out on the ice to move nets for the Zamboni machine during hockey games, there was little enjoyment for him in his work, and he too felt restless.

So in 1974 we moved from Central California to Northern Indiana, at the encouragement of friends who were going to college there. We were certainly ready for a change after a year of dissatisfaction. I was 22 years old. Our good friends Jana and Jim were working in Northern Indiana with a former priest named John who was an early and vigorous proponent of services and rights for the disabled. Jim and Jana were group home parents for developmentally disabled individuals while finishing their college degrees. They both went into special education work, each progressing to have long and illustrious careers. In those early days, their combined enthusiasm and that of their mentor John swept both my husband and me up into this work, although I had no realization that this was a historic time in disability rights. I was young and naive, of course, but idealistic and hard-working, and finally I had fallen into work that would give me a sense of fulfillment, as well as a paycheck. And yes, I would repeat that I "fell into" this work.

The paycheck was meager the first year. I worked full days as an aide in a preschool for developmentally disabled children and I earned approximately $3,000 for twelve months. My husband began working as a workshop supervisor for adults with disabilities. He earned twice my salary (working with children always seems to be associated with lower pay), so our household income that year was just about $9,000. This sounds like a paltry income now, yet at the time we felt positively middle class! Our life in Northern Indiana was a great adventure for us personally, as we experienced a very different environment and lifestyle from California. We gardened with friends, fixed up old houses together, and generally lived in close community with other like-minded young people, celebrating life. Our lives were low-key, with time spent on front porches and farms, sharing big dinners, in downtown pubs, and at occasional blue grass festivals. Once or twice a year we would head into Chicago for an urban experience, walking the lake-side avenues in the wind or shopping at Marshall Fields at Christmas-time.

But much of our life centered around work, this new cause, this new battle for human rights. It felt revolutionary, and it fed my sense that Special Education was something worthy of my energy and passion.

It was 1974. I spent the next thirty-eight years in Special Education.

Work Résumé

1974–1976	Preschool Aide, Association for Disabled Citizens in Northern Indiana
1976–1979	Teaching credential and Masters degree in Special Education, Indiana University
1977–1979	Infant Stimulation teacher, Association for Disabled Citizens, Northern Indiana
1979–1981	Education and Handicap Coordinator, Head Start program in Central California
1981–1997	Special Day Class teacher, public school district in Central California
1997–1998	General Education Kindergarten teacher, public school district in Central California

Work *Résumé*

1999–2012	Resource Specialist, public school Bay Area California.
June 2012	Retirement from teaching
June 2012	Beach time
July–August 2012	Intense closet and garage clearing
September 2012	First of many post-retirement trips across America
October 2012	Creative Writing career begins

One

We Are Only as Strong as Our Weakest Link

It was 1974. If I am going to be absolutely honest, my first day working with the children at our special needs pre-school was shocking. The thought that hovered in my mind that day was that surely these children, and their families, would have been better off if the children had been aborted. But something compelled me to stick around to gain the first of many lessons. This decision made all the difference in my career and certainly in my life.

Our preschool consisted of two classes, two teachers, two aides. All the children were taught in one big light-filled, color-filled classroom, brand new and attractive. I was one of the aides and worked with a teacher only a year or so older, named Kasey, who soon became a great friend. In our charge were twelve children with profound disabilities; two-thirds were non-ambulatory, and the other third were quite language disabled and cognitively delayed. Some of our children could not sit up without support, several were blind, and a few had severe brain damage so they would respond like infants at best, more reacting to a stroke on the cheek or a squeeze of the hand. We had children whose brains were very small due to hereditary birth defects or extreme trauma before or at birth. We had children who had suffered devastating brain injury due to illnesses and high fevers, car accidents or falls. We had children whose pre-natal health was damaged due to maternal drug or alcohol abuse. Of our children who were mobile, none could use speech or show much understanding of spoken language. One girl, a gorgeous blond named Ginger, would run around wildly with a big wooden spoon in her hand tapping it on every surface (even once on my nose, oh the pain). Her happy laughter was infectious. Another beautiful girl ran around on tip toes, crying softly, looking frightened, her long dark hair streaming behind her as she tore pieces of tissue paper into shreds. She was my Ophelia. (A tragic postscript on this little girl: Just like Shakespeare's Ophelia, this little one drowned in a creek a year after she left our classroom.)

This was the group of children that I saw that first day, just about a year after I left my last intellectually demanding philosophy, literature, history, communication, and sociology classes at college. Six hours a day I now shared charge of this class of preschoolers. I was stunned that first day, and initially abortion did cross my mind.

But I was also young. And I adapted quickly, particularly under the tutelage and example of compassionate and spirited Kasey. She loved these children, each one of them, and within a short time, I did also. Love and loving can be contagious. She treated me as a full partner and I blossomed in this unexpected environment. This was the beginning of a transformative new outlook for me.

I learned to do the therapy my non-ambulatory children needed to keep their limbs from atrophying and to keep their legs and arms from contracting and becoming stiff. I learned that if you stroked beautiful blind Mason's cheek, he would smile a smile so delightful and so genuine that everyone around him would feel happy. He laughed when we sang to him, helped him stand up and put his legs through the walking motions. His adoring mother was coping bravely. She knew the anguish of having "lost" her gorgeous nine-month-old healthy baby boy to encephalitis, but we staff were able to accept him as he was now at age three, and focus on his beautiful spirit. He made us happy with his blind but sparkling brown eyes.

Some of our children were happier than others. Some seemed very unhappy, so we worked all the harder to find something to bring them pleasure. We sang songs. We fed them tasty food, patiently mashing ingredients and slowly feeding those who had trouble swallowing. We played in the sand; we went outside and felt the warm summer breezes and the cold snow of winter. We played in the water. We took the children to the horseback therapy ranch. We chanted, sang, and moved with them; we touched them.

Each child became a cherished individual with personalities I had not noticed the first day. Almost each child brought joy to those around him or her. Sadly, there were one or two children who seemed beyond our ability to reach. We couldn't seem to lead them to a place where pleasure could be found. One little boy named Dennis I will always remember with a special pang.

He had microcephaly, born with a very small brain. He was tiny and would never grow big. He was always unhappy. He tried to chew up his hands and arms, and we finally had to put restraints on his arms so he could not bite himself so severely. His doctors worked to find a medication that might help him be calm. But in the two years I worked with him, he never found peace or pleasure as far as I could see. Unlike Dennis however, most of our children found happiness in the little enchanted classroom kingdom with Kasey and me.

Across the room, our sister class was full of children who were all able to use language: children with Down syndrome, various degrees of Cerebral palsy, or other known or unknown diagnoses. (If any of these terms look unfamiliar, I have provided a helpful glossary of special-education terms in the back of the book.) It was a delightful group of preschoolers, and our two classes often joined in spirited singing or story telling sessions or games and activities. All our children were individuals, and all of them were unique and loved, usually dearly loved by their families and always by us, the staff.

After working with these courageous and innocent little people who were completely dependent upon their caregivers, family, school and medical team for their lives and survival, I found myself moved to a new definition of strength. The old adage *We are only as strong as our weakest link* had new meaning to me. My take on it was this: We are only as strong as how well we support and take care of our weakest link. This meant children and elderly in general of course, but it specifically meant those human beings who through no fault of their own, entered this world with brains and/or bodies that could not function independently. How we look after these people and provide care for them, as well as how we respect their personhood and honor what they give back, is the test of how strong we are as persons or a society.

The two years where I served and delighted in a group of children that society would call "the least of these," transformed my life and revolutionized my thinking. The experience became absolutely central to my philosophy of life, teaching me that how we treat and respect the "least of these" is the mark of how evolved we are. We are only as great as the greatness we put into caring and honoring those who are the weakest among us. And moreover, we are given vast emotional return value from these individuals. It was the most appropriate beginning to my new career.

Two

No Place for Show Boating

After two years of working very happily as an aide, I took the advice of my teacher and went back to school to get a teaching credential. She reminded me that I was enjoying my aide job because she gave me free rein and responsibility. She was right of course; my happiness in my job would in large part be determined by the generosity and personality of whatever teacher I would be assigned to assist. Spending those two years as a teacher's aide was invaluable for me in my later years. Because I had been treated with such respect as an aide, it was always a reminder to me to do the same for those paraprofessionals who worked with me in the decades to come. While working at the paraprofessional level, I was given a chance to grow and learn and take responsibility, to use my creativity and ideas, and I always tried to take that philosophy into my classrooms through the years. I have had the privilege of working with many bright, caring, loyal, and trusted teacher's aides.

In 1976, I went back to school to earn my teaching credential and begin my master's degree program in special education, giving me the opportunity to volunteer in special classrooms and to do internships under master teachers. On these occasions, I could focus on one child and spend a great deal of one-on-one time with a student. I sometimes felt proud of how I could do all kinds of magic with a student, helping them light up and perform a skill at a higher level than ever before. Although I hope I did not appear smug, I will admit that I felt quite successful in what I could bring forth with a student.

I recall the day when I had my humbling moment. I was working with a non-ambulatory child in the corner of a classroom, and things were going very well; she was responding with animation and doing more verbalization than we had ever heard before, and showing more fine motor dexterity than ever before. The teacher who was teaching the rest of her class came over and watched for a moment in silence. Then she stated with some weariness in her voice, "Try doing that and managing the rest of the class at the same time." Not perhaps the most encouraging or generous way for a teacher to thank an intern, but even though I had never said anything derogatory about the teacher or her methods, inside my heart I knew I was full of self-righteousness. It hurt to hear her words but it was very important for me to take them in.

I remembered that experience in the years to come when I was in charge of running an entire classroom with students who had many different needs. I tried to thank my volunteers and interns and all the specialists who could come in and work individually with a student to bring out the best in that child. I appreciated them greatly and tried to keep an eye on my ego to make sure I wasn't feeling sorry for myself.

As a specialist or volunteer, there is no place for show boating. A teacher has a big job to plan, run, and manage an entire classroom all day long, and when you have the opportunity to work one-on-one, take advantage of it, but never forget whose classroom you are in, and how hard that teacher is working to plan and care for her/his students.

Conversely, every member of the team who comes into a classroom is important for the well being of the students and is necessary to make progress happen. As a teacher there is no place for ego issues. You are in charge absolutely, but it takes a village, and the bigger and better that village is, the more the students will benefit. Youthful enthusiasm and talent should be valued. Take the high road. Be grateful.

Three

M&Ms Are For Parties

I spent three years in total at Indiana University, one year full time to get my teaching credential and two more years part time to finish up my Master's degree in Special Education.

Like all the intense and full stages of my life, I have to look back in awe at all I accomplished during this time. When I finished my teaching credential and was hired as an Infant Stimulation teacher in a county Association for Disabled Citizens, I worked each day from 8:00 to 5:00 (7:00 a.m. to 6:00 p.m. including the hour commute) and then several days a week there were night classes at the University. I finally drove 30 miles home after 10:30 at night, sometimes through snow and ice, to drop into bed and turn around and start over again the next day. I know this is a way of life for millions of young men and women working and going to school today as I did in the 1970s, perhaps even raising kids as well. With full appreciation for the energy and exhaustion this time of life entails, I take my hat off to all of us.

Despite the busyness of this time, I enjoyed being a student and learning about the many different syndromes, medical disorders, and diagnoses, as well as developmental learning and teaching methods. It was the beginning of my fascination with how our brains work and how we humans learn.

I also learned what I didn't find rewarding. I worked as a Teaching Assistant for a professor in Special Education. She was working on a doctorate degree. Her thesis required collecting data and coming up with results. I liked this woman quite a lot, and it certainly was a better part-time job than many other graduate students found. But I came to discover that I did not enjoy painstaking research involving children in precisely staged conditions with various types of rewards and feedback (including the ever popular M&Ms). After all these years, I do not remember what she was studying. But I do recall concluding that this type of research did not interest me in the least, and that I would never pursue a Ph.D. degree in Special Education if this kind of work was required. It was not just the tedious nature of the data collecting and the boring technically written papers that bothered me; it was that it was hard for me to see how these experiments directly benefited the children.

I guess this distaste reflects, and perhaps not favorably, my own lack of interest in research detail. My global and holistic approach was most satisfying and successful for me, even if it wasn't always as data driven. I hope that despite this, my students benefited from my approach, and that I touched something deeper in their souls.

Having confessed this preference, I nonetheless spent a career in Special Education writing measurable goals and objectives to show accountability and to measure what sometimes were small increments of growth. I constantly wrestled with my boredom with this minutia even though I understood that it was important to identify exactly what our next step needed to be. And although it sounds contrary to what I have written here, I always loved doing assessment, not so much for the numbers I could gather but for the observations I could make about how a child was thinking and going about tasks

So what was the lesson I first learned when I was giving M&Ms to students as reinforcements for my professor's data collection? I learned that there would always be a tug of war inside me between what was required of me and how I really wanted to spend my teaching time. I learned that I had to buck up and try to make the endless paperwork as meaningful as possible for the good of the students and for my own peace of mind. I learned that being burdened with this minutia and data collecting was the price of being a teacher (rather than being a paraprofessional). And I learned early on that I could not get excited about this aspect of Special Education. Finally I learned in time that this attitude on my part would keep me from going to the "top of my field."

After my first two years of bliss working in our preschool, I learned that there was an aspect to the work that was distasteful to me, and did not speak to my essence. And I learned that it was okay, that there would be plenty of reward to feed my soul, and that as in any line of work, there was a part of Special Education that simply had to be done with as much professional skill and lack of complaining as possible.

Nonetheless, I still believe M&Ms are best for eating for pleasure, not research.

Four

"I Don't Know"

After earning my Special Education credential, I was hired by a nearby county-wide Association for the Disabled. Working as a home-based Infant Stimulation teacher from 1977 through 1979, I spent each day in homes in several communities of Northern Indiana, traveling from poor apartments to lovely homes on the river, to middle class neighborhoods and apartments. I loved this work. Based out of our school site at an old Catholic church school, my sister teachers and specialists were kindred spirits: positive, passionate, idealistic, and skilled in their respective fields of speech, language, physical and occupational therapy, social work, and education.

My job was to go into homes and work with the babies and toddlers who had been either diagnosed with a "disability" or were at risk due to birth or illness traumas. While it was tremendous fun to stimulate the little ones towards their developmental milestones, the time I spent with the parent (usually but not always it was the mother who was home) often turned out to be more significant. Unfortunately, the mother was sometimes isolated with a child whose disability may have kept her home-bound because of health concerns or behavioral issues. The saddest situation was when the parents found themselves ostracized from their own family and friends because of others' discomfort with the child's disability. At times, my weekly visit was a lifeline of social and emotional connection, as well as practical help and training with their child. Then again, I also had many families who were strong and flexible enough to embrace their child wholly into their family life with extended family support as well. As a young teacher, I learned a great deal from these strong families. And in truth, I learned a lot from the families who struggled, too.

One family lived in the shadow of a prestigious university. The parents were both bright young professionals in the academic world, and were lovely people who were very concerned about their only son, two years old. His disability was not a common one, and they had a lot of questions for his doctors and for me.

One week his grandparents were there when I arrived for my weekly visit. They too were highly educated professionals from another university out of state. The grandfather asked me a question regarding his beloved grandson. While I don't remember the question, I do remember that I had no idea what the answer might be. For a few seconds, which seemed like an eternity, I pondered whether to bluff my way through some sort of answer. Somehow I had the sense to just say, "I don't know, but I will look into it."

All week long I felt so inadequate. It is hard to imagine now because I have said "I don't know," so many times in the years since then. But at the time I was absolutely certain that when I returned the next week, I would find out that my little student's parents and grandparents would have decided they could never have their little boy working with such an ignorant teacher. I approached the front door with dread the next week. Marsha greeted me with a big smile and welcome, and one of the first things she said to me was this. "My dad was so impressed with you last week and how well Aiden responded to your work with him. And he was most impressed that you could say you didn't know something, and not try to bluff."

Five

How Parents Love
Their Children

When I went to work as an Infant Stimulation teacher, I was not yet a parent myself. I was 26 years old with a fresh teaching credential, in the process of earning a Master's degree. I would eventually write my Master's paper on the effect on families when a child has special needs. But when I began this particular teaching job, I was still pretty raw, and had very little idea what it was like to be a parent, much less what it was like to be the parent of a child with disability.

Fortunately, I gained experience and understanding over the next two years working intimately with parents and their babies and toddlers, right in their homes.

In terms of my own satisfaction at this time, I found it exhilarating to be able to move from home to home, three to four each day, and feel like I was being effective. I loved the challenge of adjusting from an upper-income home to a Section 8 housing apartment; from a home of a family newly from Appalachia to the home of an Italian mom who spoke very little English; from a young professional couple's apartment to a middle class family on Main Street USA. Being a people person, I loved the variety of people I got to meet and the opportunity to become part of the story of their lives.

I absolutely thrived in this work. In addition to the nature of the work being a perfect fit for my interests, the staff in our program was the best. It was really a Camelot working environment, and I would look back on it with deep fondness and a big sigh in years to come. The teachers and specialists were supportive, creative, idealistic, child oriented, dedicated, and funny. We were cheerleaders for each other and for our students.

As it was with my colleagues, on most occasions my home visits provided a bright spot in the week for my families, when I would come in with gusto and a bag of bright toys and ideas, able to fully appreciate that precious child and listen and affirm a parent who was sometimes quite isolated.

When a child is born with or develops what we as a society call a disability or handicapping condition, it is initially devastating to a family. The mother and father are never prepared for this revelation, whether they receive it in an instant when they see their newborn's obvious physically different characteristics, or the doctor tells them that their brand new baby has Down syndrome, or the distress of the birth process slowly leads to milestones not met or seizures out of control, and the child is labeled with Cerebral palsy. It is even more deceptive when their beautiful child is not able to communicate and shows behavioral sensitivities until finally the family is told their perfect baby has autism.

While the parents are never prepared for the reality (even if they had ultrasounds or amniocenteses), most parents are filled with such love for their child that they jump in and do what they need to do, but it can be lonely. Sometimes, extended family members and friends are so shocked that they back off. I will talk about that in another story.

As a general statement I will say that unless a parent has a serious mental illness, all parents love their children, including their child with a disability. That doesn't sound like such a profound discovery does it? But I learned after two years doing Infant Stimulation in the homes of families all over our county that parents show their love in many ways. Some families were mature and compassionate and had terrific ability to fold that little child into the bosom of their lives and home, and while not every day was easy, they modeled to me a remarkable acceptance and respect that moved me even at my young age.

For other families, it was not so easy. They struggled with their own feelings, yet it was clear how much they loved this little person they had brought into this world. But often the strong odds against their baby's future success were so overwhelming that I would see reactions and behavior that didn't look very loving. In time I came to see the truth of their love even when the outward behaviors told a different story.

The clearest lesson I learned was with a woman named Shirleen and her little boy Mitchell. Of all the weekly visits I made, this was one of the only stops that I came to dread. Shirleen was a single mom of indeterminate age who lived in a very poor housing project with multiple children running wildly around in the parking lot and young men lounging around the project giving off vibes that were at least disrespectful if not threatening. Once inside Shirleen's apartment, I could be sure that I would find numerous unexplained folks sleeping on the sofa and wandering in and out. I could also be sure that it would be way too hot in the apartment. Without having to worry about the heating bill in public housing, the families tended to keep it warm enough to wear summer shirts and dresses and the kids often wore diapers only. Coming from the Indiana winter weather outside, I would have to unwrap caps, scarves, coats and sweaters to swelter and survive for my hour visit. I was out of my element, and inside another culture.

Shirleen would open the door for me without a greeting, without a smile, without an invitation to come in. Here is where a degree of bluntness and bravado came in. When I was given this lack of welcome my first visit, even though she knew who I was and why I was there, I just entered and started playing with Mitchell. In all my subsequent visits, I just visualized that she had spread her arms wide to welcome me, and I ventured inside the apartment with an enthusiasm I really didn't feel, and courage I lacked.

Mitchell was a little Buddha baby. He sat solid and unruffled in one position for hours at a time. He was a good sitter; cross that milestone off his developmental checklist. But that was it. He simply stared at the TV, which was always on. While I asked for the TV to be turned off, it wasn't always done, so my strategy was to put my body in front of his gaze, and despite his irritation with this, begin to play with him, encouraging him to move and exercise. I used toys that I brought because there were almost no toys in his home. Sometimes, I would engage one of the other random children passing through to play with us. And while I labored to stimulate this little guy to move, to play, to do something, his mom stayed in the other room or on the sofa with her eyes on the TV. At some point in our time together, I would try to get her involved in either conversation or in the playtime. I would talk to her about Mitchell and our goals and hopes for him, about what next small steps he could be taking, but I never got a response beyond a rough murmur.

I had no sense that I was being successful with Mitchell, and I was absolutely certain that I was making no progress in getting to know Shirleen. I felt quite incompetent. I had been so proud of how I could adapt my style and approach to meet the needs of all the various families I served, but I had clearly struck out with Mitchell and Shirleen. It was not a good feeling, and I picked the experienced brain of my partner Jan for ideas.

But before we could come up with a new strategy, one day the phone rang at work during my office hours. Much to my shock, it was Shirleen. I didn't even know that she knew my phone number. I didn't even think she knew or cared what agency I represented. But she called me to give me this exciting news: Mitchell had taken his first steps!

Obviously, I was thrilled for Mitchell, but the bigger lesson came through to me powerfully. Shirleen loved her baby but she hid behind a persona formed in response to her distrust of outsiders and professional folks like me. I often felt like a damn fool in her presence. But somehow my enthusiasm, plus all those hours of genuine instruction I had given her son, and my feeble attempts to engage her and show my concern for her, had not been ignored or missed by Shirleen. When the great day came and Mitchell took his first steps, she needed to share it with someone who would care about Mitchell in a very special way. She needed to burst out her pride (and her hidden worry) for her son so badly that she found my phone number and took the time to call me, not wanting to wait until my next week's visit to share the news.

I came to understand that all parents love their children but they show it in many different ways. It was my job as an educator to really *see* and *believe* that this was true and then find a way to help these parents discover an outlet to express their love.

I also came to see that this maxim was true not just for parents of adorable little preschoolers but for parents of scruffy ten year olds and defiant teenagers as well. It was my job as an educator to find that truth in each and every parent who let me be his/her child's teacher.

Six

Children Die

I had little in my life experience to prepare me for the deaths of children. My mom had a younger brother who died early in life, back in the 1920s in rural California. I had also heard stories from my mother-in-law. She was one of seven surviving children out of thirteen born in the 1920s and 1930s in a small prairie town. The other six babies all died before the age of two years.

But it was the 1970s. At this early stage of my life, years before I became a mother myself, I really could not wrap my mind around what losing a child meant to a family, to a mother and father. In the years since the birth of my own two sons in the 1980s, I have thought long and hard about those six Canadian babies and the effect their loss must have had on the rest of my mother-in-law's family. I have studied the photo of my own grandmother as she stands behind the tiny casket, surrounded by the rest of the grief-stricken family. The sorrow on her face is palpable. I can feel her sorrow traveling through the years from that day her little son was buried to me this day. But in the 1970s when I began my career, I had no point of reference for the death of children.

In time, I came to understand, if not totally accept, that many of the little ones I worked with, both at our Preschool and later in our Infant Stimulation program, were children who were not just disabled cognitively and/or physically, but many were also medically fragile. Some of these children would never have survived birth or infancy in historical days of more primitive medical proficiency. Medical issues were very real for some of the children: seizure disorders, heart ailments, breathing issues, organ weaknesses, choking propensities, brain tumors, feeding difficulties, allergies, genetic immune disorders, and more.

These students' parents had had an unwanted crash course in life and death during the days and weeks in the hospital with their precious children. Most of them very quickly became veterans of the crisis, competent and practical, because life had dealt this set of cards to them. It is what you do for your child; you step up to the plate for whatever is needed. I noticed for the first time that while one parent looks for a play group, buys bright toys for their toddler and laughingly complains of lack of sleep, another parent spends hours regulating medications, keeping track of seizures, sucking fluid from throats, doing exercises with stiff legs and arms, learning to give injections, and holding their screaming child while he or she has medical procedures completed by a doctor or nurse. Meanwhile, the parent's heart is breaking but he or she does not have time or the luxury to dwell on the sadness. Regardless, the heartache is there, for dads and moms, and extended families too.

My students' parents took their children to places like Riley Hospital in Indianapolis, hospitals in Kalamazoo, or Chicago Shriners hospital and clinics. All of these places were hours away from the towns where I worked and my families lived. I observed for the first time what it was like for parents to leave their normal life (family, gardens, housework, other children, jobs, social groups) and drive hours to spend nights on a chair beside the bed of a sick baby or toddler. Their fatigue and sense of displacement was huge. For those parents who had other children in the family, it was a time full of guilt at not being able to give equal time to all their brood. And marriages and relationships were hit hard. In fact, it was clear to me that when there was a special needs child in a family, and especially when the child had medical needs, a good strong relationship, although still shaken, often became stronger, and a tenuous relationship tended to dissolve and break up. I saw it over and over again.

What crossed my mind during those days was that there should be someplace for families to stay overnight and rest for at least a few hours when they had to travel far from home with their ill children. Some found relatives to stay with (not always a restful, safe sanctuary), and others who could afford it would pay for a hotel. But most of the parents slept nights on chairs by the bed of their child. And often because someone had to stay home and go to work and get the older children off to school, one parent, usually the mother alone sat by that hospital bedside, exhausted, sick with worry, or numb with too many emotions. I thought to myself, why couldn't there be some convenient and supportive place for these families to use as a home base?

While I was thinking these thoughts, others were doing something about it. It was not too many years after this that the Ronald McDonald Houses started opening their doors near hospitals across the country to fill this very need. What a gift these houses are.

The lessons were coming in bucketfuls to me now—

Life is not fair, but to waste energy and angst on that thought does not help anyone make it down their path, child or adult.

Ordinary people can do heroic work when life calls them to do so.

Even those who are dealing with life and death need occasions to laugh and be light-hearted when possible.

Exhaustion and worry can take a terrible toll.

And, the most difficult lesson I learned: Children die sometimes.

In my five years in Indiana we lost children. Sometimes, it was an overnight surprise and sometimes it was a death we could see was coming. I am amazed that I can still remember some names through the years: Debby, Rochelle, Beth, Lenny, Manny, Sandra, and I know there were more. Each of these children gave a remarkable attempt at life. While each one required great diligence and often around-the-clock care from their parents, he or she also gave love and happiness in the short years they were granted. Such strong little spirits were embedded in bodies that were struggling valiantly to live. Almost forty years later as I write each name, I can see each smile. And I can remember the dignity and love of each parent.

While every one of these children has a story, the one I want to tell here is Lenny's because this little boy needs to have a tribute written and this little boy taught me a big lesson about the vast capacity of the human spirit. I also want to share Lenny's story because only he of all the children mentioned above did not have a competent mom or dad who stepped up to the plate. Yet, I do believe in my heart that his mom loved her little boy in her own way, and experienced true sorrow at his death.

Lenny entered our preschool classroom one winter day. He was carried through the door in his car seat in the arms of a strong, friendly bus driver with a hearty laugh. So Lenny came into the room with a smile on his rather dirty face. His face froze as he took in the bright colorful toys and posters, the sunshine streaming in through the large windows, the sand box, the books, the smiling faces of the teachers, and the number of children running around. Lenny was three and a half years old, and he had clearly never experienced such a setting before. After a moment's hesitation, he broke into a contagious laughter, pure and loud. I don't know if I have ever seen before or since such delicious joy expressed. That was our introduction to Lenny, and he remained a delightful happy spirit every day he spent with us.

Lenny's car seat, loaned to him for his travel to school, soon began arriving in our classroom filthy with food bits and cockroaches. We did not have an on-site lunch program and the lunches his mother provided were unappetizing to our taste, usually a slice or two of white bread with a hunk of questionable looking baloney inside. We often slipped him something we had brought from home to supplement his own lunch. Both his dietary deprivation and the hemiplegic cerebral palsy that did not allow him to walk or even crawl normally, sadly led to very poor bowel functions. When we cleaned his diapers, it was foul beyond belief. We all took turns, but even though we were diaper veterans, we had to valiantly try to keep from gagging. Poor child. He knew it was offensive and that we were in distress at those moments, and the shame in his eyes was so touching to us that we did our best to learn to mask the almost involuntary physical reaction to the smell.

To the best of my knowledge, Lenny had not been discovered by any educational or special needs programs earlier in his life. This was the 1970s and he was a child of extreme poverty. It was not uncommon that children fell between the social service cracks. That is why he did not have infant intervention by a teacher or a physical or occupational therapist or a speech pathologist until he came to our program at age three and a half. Earlier intervention might have made a difference for his mobility and speech. He lived with his young mother (fourteen years old at his birth) who herself had some special learning needs. While our social worker visited Mom at home, I don't believe we ever did get her into our center for a visit. Somehow, Lenny had come to possess his beautiful happy spirit and I like to think his mother may have had a similar positive outlook, but I will never know. I do know that Lenny thrived with our teaching, the work of our many therapists, our stimulation, and activities like horseback riding. And he gave back happiness every single day.

Fast forward several years. I had moved on to get my teaching credential and then worked as a home-based Infant Stimulation teacher for two years. After this my husband and I moved from Indiana back to Central California. I had taken a position with Head Start in a small town as an Education and Handicap Coordinator. One day, I received a letter in the mail including a newspaper clipping from a former work mate in Indiana. It contained one of the saddest news articles I have ever read. It was about Lenny.

Lenny was eight years old by this time but according to the article, he still was not ambulatory except by dragging himself on the floor with his good arm and pushing with his good leg. Lenny and his toddler sister were home alone with a five year old neighbor in their apartment unit. Mom was not there, nor was any other adult in the apartment. The five year old boy was playing with matches. The bed that they were sitting on caught on fire. Compounding the tragedy, underneath the bed were many plastic bags of clothing that created thick fuel for the flames. The five year old ran away. And the younger sister was also able to get away, although she suffered smoke inhalation from the fire and had to be carried out by the fire fighters. But Lenny never made it. A fire fighter, broke down in tears as he reported that he could see Lenny through the smoke dragging himself away from the fire, but no one could rescue him.

It was difficult not to feel angry. If I ever believed that goodness was rewarded, that innocence had a safety net of protecting angels, that we could save all the children of the world, I was released from those illusions at Lenny's pathetic death.

It didn't take long, though, for me to change my outlook, because there was nothing I could do to change what happened to Lenny. I had done my best while I knew him to give his life some happiness and stimulation for six hours each day. But I could do nothing to change the circumstances of his birth, or to chastise his mother for leaving her children home alone. In the end I took a page from Lenny's book, my young wise teacher, and instead of being consumed with anger, I took Lenny permanently into my heart as a model for the enormous capacity of the human spirit in the face of overwhelming odds. I will never doubt that it is possible to find something positive in the worst of situations because I have known Lenny. And of course, it is one of the reasons why I am such a supporter of early intervention and parent training for young mothers, as well as family planning support for young people.

If I learned many lessons from the special needs children and their parents during those five years in Indiana, I learned even deeper lessons from those children who left us too soon.

Seven

"They Like My Baby!"

When a child was referred to our Infant Stimulation program, it would be by a pediatrician or a social worker, or sometimes parents got wind of us and sought us out themselves. We always did an intake evaluation to see if the child could benefit from our free services under the auspices of the Association for Disabled Citizens.

We would gather together as specialists to greet the parent and child, and then the parent would leave the baby or toddler with us while she or he would go down the hall to have a cup of coffee and a chat with our social worker. The evaluation was done by a team consisting of our Occupational Therapist, Physical Therapist, Speech and Language Pathologist, and two Educational Specialists. It sounds laborious, but in fact, with a baby it is mostly about how the baby plays, and it involved sitting on the carpet with blanket and toys. Through engaging in play with the child and observing how the baby used his body and how she played in the settings we created, we could determine how milestones were being met, what kind of language patterns and cognitive skills were developing, and how large and fine motor skills were coming along. We had developed charts of timelines to use for comparison, and we observed not just the "what" of a child's play, but the "how" as well.

By the time we had spent some time with a baby, we had a pretty good idea if the child was close to meeting milestones or was delayed in one area or another. We also gained some insight in how the child went about play. For example, perhaps the child could place pegs in a peg board but displayed a tremor when doing so, or needed repetitions or modeling to be successful. We compiled our assessment then wrote goals and developed a program for the child.

Meanwhile, the social worker was getting to know the parent and learning what assistance, practical or emotional, this particular parent could benefit from if they decided to go forward with our program.

This was very enjoyable work for me and I sometimes couldn't believe I was getting paid for this job. (By this time in 1977, my pay as a certificated special education teacher in the state of Indiana netted me about $7,000 for a twelve month working year, which felt like riches after my paraprofessional salary of the previous years.) We staff developed excellent eyes for observation of baby and toddler play and it was exciting to begin to understand how children develop as learners, with so much unfolding between birth and age three. And we learned what a detriment it was to be delayed, how some babies needed to be specifically taught some skills whereas other babies would just pick up these skills through normal development. There were many lessons for me as I enjoyed myself with this fascinating evaluation process, but this chapter is about an even more important lesson.

A mom in her twenties came in to our evaluation group one morning, bringing her baby of about nine months old. He was happy to be left with us so after a short time she took a break and went down to chat with our friendly social worker and have a cup of coffee. She apparently opened up as she talked and was no doubt very grateful to have someone with whom to share her story. She tearfully explained how ever since the birth of her baby and the doctor's assessment that there was some degree of brain damage, her family and friends had deserted her. Clearly, they did not know what to do or say to her, and being uncomfortable, they had made themselves scarce or made inappropriate comments which wounded this woman. Her husband worked long hours, and she spent most days alone at home with her baby. She was filled with all the love any mother has for her baby, but she also worried and felt full of guilt and mixed feelings. Her pediatrician had told her about our organization and so here she was.

Meanwhile, we had a great time playing with her little boy. He was full of smiles, easy going, and while somewhat delayed, had so much going for him. This little guy seemed like he was starting to catch up with basic developmental milestones, and he possessed a great sparkling personality. We staff predicted among ourselves that he would greatly benefit from our program, and would put his whole energetic self into therapy and instruction. Our assessment was positive.

When his mom came back after an hour to collect her little boy, she listened while we explained what we had found and showed her the things he could do that were encouraging and normal. I must also add that we were an enthusiastic bunch of specialists and very approachable. The mom listened to us and thanked us, greatly excited to have her boy start working with us. Our social worker gave her a ride home and later reported back to us what happened. As they drove away from our school, the mom burst into tears, happy tears of release and relief. What she managed to say in the midst of her sobbing was this: "They like my baby!" and again, "They like my baby!"

Not having a child yet, I had never thought about what it is to be a young parent. But normally a new baby brings about a huge amount of attention from family, friends, and strangers. No one is shy. Family gather around and want to hold the baby and talk about whose side of the family he or she resembles. Stories are shared of other babies. Comparisons are made of family traits. The mother and father hear how beautiful the baby is, how smart, how clever, how adorable. Photos are taken. Gifts are received. Grandparents fight for babysitting opportunities. Strangers on the street stop and admire the baby. The parents themselves dream of what the baby will do and be. The whole world loves a baby, right?

But for this woman there was none of the above. There were no doting grandparents, uncles, aunts, or neighbors, or even friends. They had disappeared. Her loneliness was extreme. Her love for her baby was as big as any mama's, but she was fragile and without support, and felt it like a crushing weight. So when she came into our school, saw our pleasure in her baby, and heard the encouraging and positive things we had to say, she was overwhelmed by something very primal. "They like my baby. They like my baby."

I never forgot that experience, or her words. My lesson was clearly that all the parents I would meet needed at a very deep level to know that the professionals who worked with their child did, in some way, like their child. Through the years, I usually found this easy to do since most kids are likable and offer much love, affection, curiosity and life spirit; however, I will admit that occasionally I had to search long and hard to find that scrap of human appeal, that tiny bit of beauty in a student, so that I could share my honest appreciation with the parent. When I became a parent myself in later years, I was reinforced how important this was. No parent should ever have to cry out in surprise and relief, "They like my baby!" It should be a birthright and, if sadly, the parents receive it from no one else, then they absolutely must from the special education professionals in their life.

Eight
Take a Step Back

Once again, I needed to find employment. We had moved back to Central California, I reluctantly leaving behind my beloved job in Northern Indiana. At this time, I took a double job as an Education and a Handicap Coordinator with Head Start because of a long phone conversation with Lilia, the head of the rural county Head Start program. I have made many important decisions in my life based on relationship and this one was based on the confident feeling I had after an hour on the phone with Lilia. And my instincts were absolutely right on with Lilia. She was a stellar director and a very fine person as well.

Sadly, Lilia left Head Start after my first year due to a family crisis and the entire staff missed her very much. Miranda took her place and we all felt the change and the loss of Lilia's calm capable leadership that instilled trust in everyone she met. Miranda had come up through the ranks of Head Start, beginning as a parent herself. She had gone to college and educated herself while being a single mom and living in poverty. Lilia had believed in her, and Miranda was a truly quality individual who paid back the faith Lilia had in her. When Lilia left, Miranda was made director.

Miranda was not confident, although she knew the program backward and forward, and no one cared more for the children and staff, or believed more strongly in the principles of Head Start. And no one else, certainly not Lilia who came from Los Angeles, knew the town and people and the whole county area, as well as Miranda. Still, she did not exude competency in those early days. I was mourning the loss of Lilia, and perhaps Miranda was as well. And I was viewed as a bit of an outsider myself, having been with the program only one year at that time, having settled in a nearby larger city instead of the immediate Head Start area, and hailing from another state, Indiana. (The fact that I had been born and raised in a small Central Valley town just 70 miles away didn't seem to register at first.) Having an advanced degree made me more "suspect" initially, even though higher education was a dream for many of our Head Start staff and parents. It was a confusing scenario for us all, but I had worked very hard through that first year to develop mutual respect and affection with all the staff. I had begun to feel that wonderful sense of belonging, but when Lilia left, my situation felt precarious.

My conversations and encounters with Miranda became uncomfortable. I felt like I had to explain myself and redouble my efforts to present good reports. I had to repeat myself often. I felt disadvantaged, at odds, unappreciated, and defensive which had never been the case when Lilia had been there. It was not pleasant. I even wondered if it was time for me to leave. But I believed in the Head Start program. I had worked so hard to belong that resigning at that moment seemed to fly in the face of all my efforts.

Finally one day, I had an insight. I was talking with Miranda in her office. She was ensconced behind her desk, and I was standing in front of her desk. I told her something and she replied "Huh?" I was annoyed at this unprofessional response. And then I realized that she always said that to me, and that I always reflexively repeated whatever it was I had said to her. This happened, I realized with a start, each time we talked. Every time I would repeat what I had said, and every time I felt on the defensive and like she was in a position of authority and I was insignificant. No other director or boss I had ever worked with had made me feel this way. No wonder I was uncomfortable with Miranda.

So on impulse I tried something. This time I did not repeat what I said, but instead stood there quietly waiting. Within a few seconds, Miranda had processed everything I had said, and replied to me. We smiled at each other, and I went back to my office. Something good had happened to both of us.

I understood that for whatever reason (and there were numerous possibilities), Miranda had a pattern of reacting to information in this manner. And for whatever nervous reason on my part, I always fell into the same response pattern. Once I realized this, all the accompanying emotions that overcame me in these situations simply disappeared. And I think Miranda learned something, too. She was a very smart and perceptive woman, and as I came to know her over the next year, she really did appreciate all I gave to our program in energy and guidance.

My lesson here? Take a step back, be the observer of the situation, try to separate the accompanying emotions from what might be really happening. Take a moment of silence; you never know what might happen. This lesson gave me another good year of service to this wonderful Head Start program, as well as a warm relationship with Miranda. Before I decided I couldn't make the commute anymore and changed jobs, I felt mutual love and admiration with the staff there, and especially with Miranda.

Nine

Build Realistic Hopes and Dreams

My time with Head Start as a Coordinator of Education and of Handicap services was invaluable to me as an educator and as a human being. I am grateful that I listened to Lilia on the phone, flew out from Indiana for the interview, and stuck with the experience even though it was initially very difficult for me. For the first weeks, I sobbed on that long commute to work, then after parking my car, I took a deep breath, shook my tears out of my face, went in and faced the day. I missed my coworkers in Northern Indiana, the lovely children and families with whom I had formed ties. I missed knowing exactly what I was doing. And I missed being surrounded by goodwill, praise, compliments, laughter, collegiality, confidence, and acceptance. I learned these very things were there for me in Head Start, as well, but I had to earn those perks. So I set to and did the best I could do. I gained a great new friend, Nina, our Nutrition Coordinator, who shared my commute as well as my daily angst and success. I slowly worked at building trust, reliability, and respect with the teachers and other workers of the program. And in time I came to love the Head Start program and the people who worked there.

And, as in so many circumstances, I gained from the two year experience as much as I gave. The lesson I learned from Head Start was the importance of helping parents and families become forces of change and makers of dreams for their children to lift them out of poverty into full and useful lives. The Head Start program believed that if the parents could be part of the educational process, the whole family would gain. Many of the employees of Head Start were parents who first came to parent meeting;, then they took advantage of the educational workshops and one-on-one support from established staff. For the rest of my teaching career, a center point for my teaching was the significance of the parents in my students' lives.

The other related lesson I picked up from this job is that Head Start helps children and families learn realistic goals for the future. If you grow up in poverty, and the only work or career choices you see as a youngster are to be a farm laborer or housekeeper... or, on the opposite scene, to be a celebrity who has lots of money and clout, for instance a professional football player, or a pop star, then of course the celebrity life seems more desirable. The young person may likely set some pretty unrealistic goals. True, occasionally a rock star or pro player will actually arise from the local scene, but it is a very long shot. And when it doesn't happen, or it happens short term and then is over, it is easy to sink back into the default, which is either unemployment or a hard working but low paying labor job. In light of those less-than-promising choices, unfortunately, making money by criminal means seems an appealing option.

Head Start worked hard to promote realistic goals that would bring about a good life of work and contribution, goals that would break the poverty cycle. It all started and ended with education and employment. As part of the Head Start curriculum, children and their parents were given information about realistic jobs, from teacher to doctor, including lawyer, plumber, hair dresser, taxi driver, gardener, pharmacist, shop keeper, factory worker, and many more. I hadn't realized until working with Head Start that intentionally teaching what had been missing in many lives could make a difference in the outcome. It is not easy to rise out of poverty; there are many strikes against you, but with realistic dreams, and help from friends and good educational and job assistance programs along the way, it can happen. This frame of mind needs to start young and that is what Head Start is all about: education, working together, having realistic dreams, supporting others, receiving training, providing help and guidance to others, and being an entity in the community. Head Start is a federal program conceived and funded in far-off Washington, DC, and it was political for many people but I experienced it as a powerful grassroots movement that opened connections across time and space.

I didn't stay with Head Start long, only two years. I wanted to get back into direct teaching in Special Education and stop spending so many hours on the road, but I learned a lifetime of lessons from this amazing program. So-called poverty programs have riches to teach us all.

Ten

Looking From Both Sides Now

My Head Start program was headquartered in a pretty little farm town with a charming center plaza, a theater, old stores like a popular classic soda shop, and even some Bed and Breakfast inns; this was not necessarily typical for Central Valley farm towns some of which were much grittier or depressed. When I took the job in 1979, fresh from our five-year stay in Northern Indiana, I knew of the town but had not spent time there before. There were two towns, I came to learn. The tale of two cities. As a middle-class professional I was really drawn to the picturesque attributes that money and community leaders had provided in this town. But now I worked in a low-income program serving the citizens who lived on the "other side of the tracks." I really had a foot in both cities. While my understanding grew for the folks who lived and worked in the poorer side of town, I was still a middle-class woman who could afford to shop in town and even consider buying a house on the pretty tree-lined streets.

This dilemma was illustrated by the potential building of a new K-Mart just outside the downtown area. The poorer folks of town were thrilled. They would be able to purchase more with their dollars than before and not have to drive out of town to do so. On the other side of this controversy, the small business owners and townsfolk who loved the ambiance of the small shops in the quaint main streets of town were appalled and fought the new K-Mart intrusion. Ultimately, the K-Mart was put in outside town, with a large unsightly parking lot.

This issue pointed out to me how one's perspective can determine one's opinion on an issue. While a big part of me continued to oppose the mega store coming in because of the effect on small-town merchants and the pleasing downtown atmosphere, I did need to take a minute to see how it would look different to someone trying to buy school clothes for their children on a farm laborer's income, or a house cleaner's wages, or a Head Start classroom aide's pay check. A person struggling to make ends meet cannot always afford to worry about the overall quality of life in a small town. Sometimes that feels like a luxury.

The lesson here was how important it is to walk in someone else's shoes or at least to look at the world through another's viewpoint.

At this time, I had done some traveling back and forth across the country by car and train and plane. I had been to Europe as a college student. My husband and I settled back in a larger metropolitan area when we returned from Indiana and our house was the stopping place for our friends who lived and traveled in many places in the US and Canada, and sometimes beyond. It was not that I myself was a vastly sophisticated world traveler, but my world included people who did travel extensively.

In the more rural area around our Head Start centers, as in Indiana, I met people who didn't travel, who felt that going to the larger college town twenty miles away was an excursion. I called this provincial thinking and behavior. It was not totally foreign to me because I had grown up in the 1950s and 60s in a small town. My own parents didn't travel much, however many of my other relatives did travel all over the nation and world. And with hundreds of books for my pleasure at home and at the library, I always viewed myself as part of a much bigger world.

I will qualify this even further by stating that I am certain there were world travelers among the citizens in and around my Head Start environment, and that the town held any number of residents with broad world views, but I remember in 1979 being startled by how many people in the Head Start program responded to my commute as being outrageous and treated my not being local as odd and perhaps not totally trustworthy until proven otherwise. In the Head Start program I met many people who were locally bound, which is why the coming of a K-Mart was a big deal, bringing the outside retail world to their very own town.

After working at Head Start the first year and gaining a familiarity and affection for the children, parents, staff, and people of the county in general, I took a trip east. I visited a teacher I had worked with back in Northern Indiana. Kasey was getting a nursing degree at an university in Manhattan. I had a wonderful visit and learned a great deal about New York and New Yorkers, including that many were friendly and helpful. But one thing I encountered during that vacation stuck in my head especially as

I thought about my new rural county friends in my Head Start community. While in New York, I met a roommate of Kasey's who was a nursing student too, an attractive New Yorker, sophisticated in taste and style, educated and from an upper-middle-class home. And I discovered that this young woman was also provincial.

Or at least that is what I called it, even though I don't think she would have seen it that way. But I was astonished. To this young woman, nature and the great outdoors were represented by Central Park, a great park, but hardly Yellowstone or Yosemite, or the Appalachian Trail. She had rarely been out of New York, and in fact had no real desire to go anywhere else except perhaps to London or Paris. Most perplexing and alarming, I felt she really didn't have any use for anyone who came from outside New York. This young woman was as provincial as any of the folks I had met in our Head Start program, even though it seemed to me that she had money and education enough to have risen above this limited mentality. I came home with some new thoughts.

The lesson? Sometimes the same mentality can be cloaked in many different appearances. Perhaps while in New York City I had discovered "sophisticated provinciality." And while it looked different, the effect was not much different than small-town provincial thinking.

Eleven

"They" Will Find Out I Don't Know What I Am Doing!

In 1981 I became a public school teacher. This was a huge shift for me in many ways although I certainly was not aware of the full ramifications of the change at that time. I was not quite thirty years old, and I was still making job decisions with an attitude that expressed, "I will take this job for a few years to give myself another experience in this Special Education work. Then I will move on to something new." Up to that time I had stayed no more than two years at any given job. The reason I left the Head Start program was because I was tired of commuting through the fog. I didn't know it at the time, but I would soon be having my own children, and it was a good move to reduce the number of hours I spent on the road.

Entering the public school realm offered me the good and the bad of being a public servant. Until 1981 I had known the good and the bad of private sector employment, as well as the experience of working for a federal government preschool program with enormous local flavor and direction. With the public schools I was now part of a large school system with regulations, paperwork, demands, and scrutiny. My life would be dictated by the school bell, both literally and figuratively. Along with the ball and chain of regulation, however, came an organized union that had fought for justice in working conditions for teachers, including health benefits, retirement plans, and offered legal support against punitive administrative actions. I also had, for the first time ever, a summer break and a reasonable salary

My first job with a public school district was at a central city elementary school, and I was very excited to now be working less than two miles from my home after years of commuting up to 30 miles one way through snow and ice and country roads (in Indiana) and fog and freeways and more country roads (in California).

My new job was to teach a Special Day Class for first and second and some third graders. Other than my student teaching at Indiana University, all my work experience had been with preschoolers, very different from what I was about to undertake. At Head Start I had been doing supervisory work, educational training, and Special Education Individual Education Plan (IEP) work. In the Infant Stimulation program in Indiana, I had been working in homes with toddlers, infants, and parents. As a Masters student at Indian University South Bend, I had done a variety of substituting jobs, internships, and one-on-one volunteer teaching, but I had not had my own class. And my first job had been as an aide in a free-flowing classroom. Now at my new school, I would have my own classroom within a regular elementary school setting.

Those who hired me saw me as vastly experienced, and I certainly had learned many lessons already. I was relatively mature, apparently exuding confidence and capability. Deep down however, I felt intimidated by the new situation. I had a lot to learn, and there was no other way to do it but to jump in and start trying. I was given a student teacher the second semester of the school year, and explaining what I was doing and why to this young man who came into my classroom each day, clarified my own thinking and helped me become a more intentional and thoughtful teacher.

I was still insecure however. To the best of my memory, I did not call in sick all year, not because I was never sick, but rather because I was sure that if a substitute came into my room for the day, it would be clear to the whole world that I didn't know what I was doing. I have often wondered if other new teachers have that same apprehension. I am grateful for Lynn, another Special Day Class teacher, who lent a helping hand while never making me feel inferior. Without her, I never would have known how to organize a field trip, order instructional movies, or learn the ebb and flow of a Special Education classroom in the public schools. She was only at my school for one year when I was there, but she was the perfect role model. She was friendly, confident, supportive, and positive, and she loved the students, had high expectations, and made me feel like a competent colleague. Thanks, Lynn, wherever you are now.

One day a supervisor from Special Education dropped by to give me some paperwork I needed. When these drop-in visits happen, you always hope that things are smooth and well run at that moment. The moment she happened to walk into my classroom, I was on the floor showing the children some yoga exercises. I believed strongly in the positive effect of yoga on the body and mind, of children and adults. I believed that imagery and visualizations practiced could help children in many ways. But I still wondered if perhaps my supervisor would not agree with me, and would prefer that my students be sitting at their desks quietly practicing handwriting or reading in small groups. After watching us for a few minutes, the supervisor simply dropped the file off on my desk, and walked out of the room, leaving me to question if this would reflect poorly on my job performance. Much to my relief, I found out sometime later that this supervisor was not just impressed with the overall atmosphere of relaxed yet focused students, but supported me using any (reasonable) technique which I the teacher believed would help my students, regardless of whether she herself would have used the same method.

Over and over again that first year, these incidents began to add up. And my confidence increased. It became clear to me and to my supervisors that the evidence of happy and focused students who were making progress on their goals was proof of good teaching.

Lesson? Sometimes you have to dive in, and try things, make mistakes, and learn. And seek out a fun-loving and knowledgeable colleague for practical and emotional support so you don't feel so alone. I trust that this helped me become that same kind of colleague for others in years to come.

And for Pete's sake, take your sick days when you need them!

Twelve

Come from the Love

Between 1980 and 1982, I attended some workshops that helped me explore many of the thoughts going through my mind in those days. From my current vantage point they hardly seem revolutionary, but for me at that time, what I learned became important building blocks to my developing life philosophy. I explored spirituality beyond the organized religious teaching of my childhood. Without negating any of the positive teachings with which I had been raised, these studies expanded my thinking both inwardly and globally. And for the purpose of my working life I was exposed to concepts and specifics that helped immensely. I will share an example.

One phrase coming from the workshops became a mantra for me while teaching my Special Day class: "Come from the Love." It was amazing to me how this simple phrase helped me start each day. At school, as in any work situation, I did not always automatically start every day with this high-minded loving attitude. There were days I was exhausted. There were days when I was distracted. There were days when I got into figurative wrestling matches with my most manipulative students. Days when I would feel the need to control the class, and that would get in the way of my pure motives. There were days when I wanted my teaching to look good, appear effortless, when I wanted all my subjects to bow down and respect and honor me as queen bee teacher, extraordinary entertainer, and fairy godmother all in one. The title of many a book and teacher workshop touted "classroom management," i.e. having control over a class, and as a younger teacher I took this to mean that I had to work extra hard, using prescribed specific techniques, be extremely energetic and entertaining, and by sheer force of will, obtain that good-looking classroom management.

In a class such as the one I was now teaching, the dynamics were very different than any previous teaching or work situation I had encountered. I was working with children between the ages of six and nine years, who had varying types and degrees of brain damage or learning disorders, whose home and backgrounds were quite varied, ranging from admirably healthy to very neglectful or even abusive. Achieving classroom management, what did that mean? Students not climbing on the desks and throwing furniture? Students doing everything you told them to do? Some days effective class management just seemed to happen, and other days seemed beyond my reach.

My classroom didn't often appear out of control, but I *knew* something wasn't right. I had that sense some days that I was holding on by my finger tips to have the healthy, creative, mutually satisfying learning environment that I wanted. I knew, even if my supervisors didn't, even if no one else noticed, even if all my evaluations were first rate and my principals sang my praises, I was aware that my classroom environment was not what it should be, even though I looked *good*! I knew that on a spiritual level, all was not good; my motives were not clear and pure. I was just trying to achieve control. I had lost, on those bad days, my love of the teaching. And I think it was because I had lost sight of my students and of finding love for them.

You could substitute the word respect, if love is too intimate a word or concept for you, and makes you uncomfortable. But for me, the way I learned the phrase worked the best. So every day when I would look just to the right of my daily lesson plans spread out on my desk, I saw the words, "Come from the Love" written in large letters under the glass top on my old wooden school desk. When I saw that, I reminded myself that first and foremost I needed to love all these students. And some days that was hard, when my students behaved in annoying and obnoxious ways, and were downright obstructionist to my goal of having a well-run classroom. But no matter what well-developed and sophisticated behavioral management plan I had set up, I discovered that if I didn't come from a place of love and respect for the child, it would not work.

I hope this is making you smile a little bit or shake your head in disbelief that someone almost ten years into a career would not already know this basic educational truth. Or perhaps you think this is all too touchy-feely, and all that really matters is technique and program. But if there is even one teacher out there, new or a veteran, who can relate to this, then I am happy to bare my soul and share my lessons and my experiences.

When I reminded myself that teaching was not about me, I could start on the path to becoming a better teacher. This was all an inward struggle; anyone looking in from the outside would not have noticed these subtle underlying tug-of-wars in my heart and soul. But I mention my inner dilemma because I do believe that in the long run, as well as in the short term, this was a vital realization for me! I could have struggled through a long career of teaching, looking good, but missing out on the deep joy of teaching, and doing a great disservice to my students by not creating the best environment for them. And I would have been exhausted, for all the wrong reasons.

So every morning I would look at my reminder, "Come from the Love," and then as I welcomed my students for the day, I would know clearly that the most obnoxious, unlikeable student was the one who needed the most love and understanding. That was the student who I must work extra hard to learn to know, to figure out what made him or her tick, what would motivate. And most importantly, by seeing the student first, I took myself out of the spotlight, and it was no longer all about me, about that student's behavior getting in the way of my great lesson plans, or my smooth classroom flow. Teaching was about the child, and my task was to try to help that student have a better day, to learn socially and academically something new and important.

I had another slogan right next to "Come from the Love." This too I had learned from my workshop experiences. It said, "Avoid Power Struggles Absolutely!" Learning to Come from the Love went a long way to avoiding the power confrontations, but it was a good reminder to make sure I didn't get into battles with my students. While I was the authority figure in the classroom (and as an adult I was set up to be the winner with the backing of the administration, other teachers, and usually the child's parent, too), there was still no way I "won" or anyone "won" when there was a power confrontation. Most importantly, there was no way the child gained understanding of how to deal with situations in the future, whether with me or with anyone else. All the student learned when I let a power struggle occur, was that the adult is stronger and has more outward power. So for the present time, the more aggressive or manipulative student would show his or her power by finding ways to make life for the teacher and everyone else as difficult as possible. The more docile children who cowered at the power of a teacher and never misbehaved were not learning anything about how to make their own decisions, trust their own judgment, or be assertive in a healthy manner either.

Ultimately I wanted my students to decide to follow the basic rules, get along with others, and be open for learning because they were so excited about learning that they wanted to be right on task. And it was my job to create an environment where they were loved and respected, where the learning was creative, inviting and stimulating. Can this be more difficult to achieve in a classroom where the children are challenged by issues of cognitive, physical, communication and/or social disabilities? Of course, but at the core, children are children, people are people, and all have a basic need to be valued, respected, and given the opportunity to learn and create. It is the teacher's job not to control them for six hours a day, but to foster and feed these needs. It is their due and it is so much more satisfying for everyone, even when it is a rocky road leading to that goal.

When I look back, I can see that this awareness grew in me over the years I was in the Special Day Class, particularly those first two years. And this awareness was extremely helpful when I became a parent myself in 1983 and again in 1986.

Some people, some teachers, seem to know this automatically. For whatever reason they are more highly evolved from the beginning. That was not me though. I had to learn it myself, day in and day out in my classroom arena.

If I could go home at the end of the day and say, yes, I did Come from the Love today even with young Douglas who was the oddest, most defiant and unlikeable student in the school, and if I could say upon reflection that I managed to avoid power struggles absolutely today, then that was a good day's work, and I knew I would sleep well. Tomorrow would be another day.

Thirteen

Know Your Students

Most of this memoir is about what I have learned through my work experience, and the lessons about teaching and parenting could fill many volumes. But some of these educational life lessons came from the experience of being on the other side of the parent/teacher conference table.

I have known many fine compassionate teachers who did not have children of their own. And I don't denigrate my own contribution to the families and students I served prior to becoming a parent myself at age 31. Nonetheless, I know that something changed in my teaching attitude and perhaps even my actual teaching after my first son was born in 1983. Perhaps the most vital lesson that was reinforced for me was what a difference it makes to parents to feel that their child's teacher really knows their child.

This is really the other side of the conference table from the earlier chapter entitled "They Like My Baby!" By the time I was a parent myself and began to have experiences with my own sons' teachers, I realized that this lesson needed to be fine-tuned. It was not enough to merely gush affection about a student to a parent. What was essential was for the parents to see that you really did know their child, your student. There is a magical moment between parent and teacher when it becomes clear that not only does the teacher like, enjoy, and respect the child, but also truly knows who that child is, what makes him/her tick, what his/her learning styles are, what his/her preferences are, what is difficult for him/her, and what comes more naturally for that child. Sometimes this means talking about a child's less productive behaviors or characteristics, ones that hinder social and academic growth. When parents fully know that you are in their child's camp, it is quite possible to discuss the whole child, warts and all.

When one of my son's teachers showed this kind of observational gift, when I could see that he or she took the time and effort to know my son, which meant that this teacher also knew each of her or his other students, I was ready to grab the hand of that teacher and partner together all year long. I would walk from those parent-teacher discussions and conferences convinced that my son was in good hands and would be getting all possible learning and growth that school year. My son would understand that his teacher and his parent presented a strong unit looking out for his best interest, behooving him to toe the line, try his best, be creative but not waste time trying manipulation.

When I look back through the years to my sons' teachers, I can remember examples that illustrated this skill of "knowing" extremely well, and unfortunately a few examples of very poor student knowledge.

I recall walking away from a primary classroom after my son's parent-teacher conference shaking my head with the awful feeling that after almost three months of school my son's teacher was searching her brain to remember who my son was! I could have cut her some slack because of the large class size of 33 students, but these overly large class sizes had never deterred other teachers from showing me by all they noticed, how well they knew my sons.

I had another bad experience of a teacher who gushed about my son all the time whenever I would talk with her. Finally about two thirds of the way through the year, I took a day off work myself to help chaperone a class field trip out of town. Spending a day with the class and the teacher opened my eyes to what was going on. On top of other dysfunctional relationships among students and between teacher and students, my son was being bullied, and the teacher didn't have a clue. She liked to charm parents with her praise of their child, but in reality she had no idea what was going on, or she chose not to see it. I paid much closer attention after that and was able to work with my son to help him deal with a situation that I had not realized existed prior to my chaperoning experience. My trust in this teacher had been shaken, although there was nothing concretely illegal or wrong with what she was doing.

The following year my son had a whole different kind of teacher, one who was on the surface wise-cracking and blunt, yet she knew each student like the back of her hand within a short time, and this was evidenced in every encounter with her students and every conversation we had. She knew what was going on in the classroom, in the lunch room and on the playground. My trust of her was great, and my son relaxed and was open to maximum learning that whole year.

I am grateful that my sons were lucky over and over again with teachers who not only knew how to teach educational concepts but also knew how to set up a learning environment that made it safe, acknowledged different learning styles and needs, and were able to know my boys. The payoff for these teachers was a more enjoyable experience with my sons (as well as with their 32 other students) and a far more productive parent/teacher relationship. This was an important lesson I learned from across the parent-teacher table.

Fourteen

The Children Still Speak to Me

So many children passed in and out of my care while I was teaching my Special Day Class. Over time, one year blended into another year, but even now some faces and names jump out into my memory. In fact there are far more than I can ever take the space to mention here.

I must speak of Craig, however. Craig was my student for two years, first and second grade. Craig was pure love and joy. His premature birth and subsequent seizures had damaged his ability to learn academics and social skills in the normal stages, and he had some unusual interests that were always front and center in his awareness. If he felt stress, his focus was particularly centered on these interests. Craig liked machines and trains but particularly he liked vacuum cleaners. And more particularly, he loved

Kirby vacuum cleaners. One year his mom had the bakery make his birthday cake in the likeness of a Kirby vacuum cleaner. His parents also had an understanding with the local Kirby shop that on special occasions Craig could come down to the shop and look and touch the Kirbys and talk to the owner about his special machine.

Our Craig also loved flowers, and he loved to make people happy. For two years hardly a school day went by where he didn't arrive with his mom or dad or grandmother, with a flower or a bouquet of flowers in hand to give me with a shy and sweet smile on his face. In the cold winter months he must have looked far and wide to find a flower he could pick for me. When our two years together were over, he and his mother gave me a Margaret Hudson sculpture of a smiling bear with an overflowing armful of roses. I still have it and it brings that generous boy and his lovely family right back into my mind. I continue to keep track of Craig and his family all these years after our time in class.

Then there was Cherry. She had a Carol Channing hair cut and great big eyes which could sparkle, but what I remember most is how they would fill with the biggest tear drops I had ever seen. These tears would hang on her eye lids for a moment and would then spill over onto her cheeks. She cried when she was confused, when things changed. Something as simple and ordinary as changing from one learning station to another could cause her such concern and confusion that she would burst into tears in the most dramatic way. When Cherry was happy, she was very happy. When she was sad, she looked distraught. Her family was patient with her, giving her love and guidance. They accepted her for own special qualities but all the while worked towards helping her be more able to function successfully in life and school.

Craig was a special boy. And Cherry was a special girl. But I had classrooms full of special children each with needs similar, or more or less pronounced, than Craig's or Cherry's. What these two children had that was unique, besides sweet dispositions, were incredible families. This was a vitally important part of Cherry's and Craig's progress and social happiness. Most all of my students' parents tried hard, and loved their child with fervor, demonstrating this in many different ways but some of these ways were more productive than others. Still I could see the love. There was timeless beauty in these parents, even those with many rough edges. But the tremendous love, maturity, and acceptance practiced in Cherry's and Craig's home were of a higher quality than most. I was in awe of what they possessed and how they raised all their children, including their Craig and their Cherry.

But did I ever have a more beautiful child than Marco? Marco was a handsome boy who had the best academic skills in my class that year or any year I taught my special Day Class. Marco had out-of-control ADHD, which had responded successfully to Ritalin. It had been a life-saving drug for him. Marco liked school so much that on mornings when his well-meaning but unreliable dad didn't get up in time, Marco would get himself up, get dressed, and sometimes even climb the fence and bars around his house to get out to the school bus. Marco was the first student I ever had who could talk to me rationally about what it felt like when he took his medication and what he felt like when he didn't. It shocks me to think that Marco would now be in his mid-thirties. I wonder what his life has been like. I can only hope that he had powerfully good teachers and other role models to help him along his way to adulthood, to help him develop that essential goodness that was inside of him, and that he stayed safe on the streets.

Lesson from my time with Craig and Cherry: I had much to learn from grace-filled loving families such as theirs. I became a better person just being in the presence of their joy and acceptance. As I read on a card once, "Some beautiful scent always remains on the hand that gives flowers."

I also see the lesson I learned from Marco and others like him who started out with no social or family advantages in life. His only advantage was a sweet and open nature, a desire to learn, and the oomph even as an eight year old to get himself into a situation where he was treated with respect and where life was happy.

There was another memorable learning experience from my time teaching my Special Day Class, this from working with students of many different backgrounds. I was long familiar with families from Mexico and Central America, especially from my time in Head Start, and I loved working with their little "mijos" and "mijas." But in the early 1980s, the school district experienced a massive influx of South East Asian families who came to Central California after the Vietnam War. Over the years, I had students from Vietnam, Cambodia, Thailand, and Laos.

The largest group of refugees who had arrived in California via the refugee camps in Thailand was the Hmong, from the mountains of Laos. As a "nation," they had been recruited by the CIA to fight along with the Americans during the Vietnam War. Naturally when the Americans left suddenly, the Hmong were in grave danger. The Hmong people escaped for their lives, leaving their homes in the mountains, fleeing through the jungles, swimming in desperation across the Mekong River into Thailand where they were safe. But safety meant years of living in refugee camps, awaiting a place to call home.

During the war and the following escapes, families were decimated through violence and illness. The father of one of my students told me harrowing stories of losing thirteen of his siblings, plus his parents, cousins, aunts and uncles. He was one of the few in his extended family who survived only to sit for years in Thailand in a camp before finally coming to America. When I made a home visit to my student Chee's home, I was shocked to see that his home was sitting across a cul-de-sac from a drug house. The first day I visited, men with shot guns were standing in the yard of that home. It was frightening for me to be there, and the father told me that he could not let his children out to play in the yard of their rental house. They had come so many miles to a strange new land, yet they had not escaped violence or the potential for violence.

74

Another Hmong family I remember was that of Bee Her. A slight boy with a willing smile, he loved to draw. I found out his father liked to draw also. I sent home bundles of old blank computer paper to Bee's dad so he would have paper to draw on. In return the father would draw pictures for me. His pictures depicted his family's escape, showing men, women, and children under the trees, traveling, running, hiding, with planes and guns firing at them from the sky, soldiers with guns amongst the trees. Those drawings showed families with babies and old grandparents swimming or taking boats to cross the heavy currents of the Mekong River. I still have some of these drawings today. I was abruptly brought face to face with what life was like for these people who had lived for generations in their mountain villages farming the land but then were brought into the war with its bitter outcome. It had only been about thirty years since the Hmong language had been put into writing and the culture shock for these people in America was tremendous. Americans did not welcome them with open arms. There was huge prejudice. But I have to compliment my school district for rising to the occasion, doing teacher education classes, raising awareness of cultural differences and expectations, and in general training teachers to help make the transition into American education as smooth as possible for our Hmong students.

Another Hmong student named Mai will always be in my memory. Mai was a little bundle of energy and full of emotions. She had learning difficulties and was not able to manage her behavior or learn in a general education classroom. In my Special Day Class she found acceptance, a pace of learning that worked for her, and understanding for her outbursts of both joy and unhappiness. She was very volatile and very delightful. Her family invited me to their home where I was treated like royalty. This same respect was given me in the homes of other Cambodian, Laotian, and Vietnamese families, too. No matter how poor they were, they would find me a chair and offer me a beautiful plate of strawberries or other fruit, plus an ice cold Coke or Pepsi. I have several pieces of beautiful Pa Ndau stitchery given to me as gifts by the Hmong women.

I learned many lessons in opening up my heart to others who had lived lives completely different from mine. The respect and importance these American newcomers held toward education made me understand all the more how we must not take educational opportunities for granted. This was a lesson that broadened my mind and understanding but also led full circle back to my own grandparents who were immigrants themselves. My grandparents worked exhausting days, struggled with poverty and misunderstandings, cherished their families and their faith. They valued education as a treasure and a privilege. They saw education as a gateway to not just a better economic future, but to a deeper understanding and enjoyment of history, literature, the sciences, religion and all of life. That same belief, of hope for the future, beyond today's basic survival, was reflected on the faces of these new immigrants from Southeast Asia.

Craig
"Some beautiful scent always remains on the hand that gives flowers."

Hmong stitchery on a shopping bag

The artist was modest. I believe he illustrated the horrors of his war experience very vividly.

Fifteen

Expect the Unexpected

I cannot leave my years in the Special Day Class behind and move on with this memoir without sharing a few more stories. Every day teaching in a Special Day Class was an adventure. And I say that with complete love and respect for my students. I am convinced that these children were heroic in their ability to make it through their days. I say that because every day is an adventure for a child with special needs as they navigate through a bewildering world. But often their responses to the world, or their defense to all that didn't make sense to them, brought about some behaviors that made each day of teaching an adventure for all of us.

There was the boy who was extremely skilled at sneaking out of the playground and running away. Our classroom was on a public school campus and back in the 1980s schools did not resemble the fortresses we often see today. There was a chain link fence that lined one edge of the playground, placed there mainly so the soccer balls would not go out on the busy avenue. And another much taller chain link fence lined the row of houses behind the play ground so neighbors didn't have to constantly retrieve balls. Gates were minimal and flimsy. It didn't take much for Douglas to slip out of the play yard and disappear. One time, he was found at a large department store a mile away. What a scary hour. I still shudder when I imagine how in the world he safely crossed two major thoroughfares.

These fences also didn't stop another of my athletic and non-verbal children from clambering to the top of the sixteen foot fence. This spectacle was made especially interesting by the fact that his other favorite activity besides climbing was stripping off his clothes. Best yet, bringing about his biggest grin, was when he could combine these activities.

Other interesting recess behaviors included a couple of children, a boy and a girl, who bonded immediately as friends. However, when I realized that part of this bonding was what they were doing together after crawling out of sight inside a huge tractor tire on the playground, I changed my assessment of the health of this friendship.

Then there was Jay. Big Jay towered over his fellow eight-year-olds. I am a tall woman but Jay and I looked each other in the eye. I never knew Jay to be violent or even aggressive, but he was very autistic. Between his size and his unusual demeanor, he was an intimidating presence on the playground. The day he fixated on an innocent second grade girl, I knew this infatuation was going to mean trouble. Unless we watched him every minute he would stalk her. The rightfully frightened child told her parents and her father angrily insisted to our principal that Jay be removed from campus. That didn't happen. Somehow we managed to help Jay eliminate if not his obsession, at least the scary behavior, and assure the girl that we would protect her from any harm. As we explained the situation to the family, the girl was easier to reassure than her father.

Inside the classroom Big Jay was capable of learning academics but when something upset him, he would get agitated and begin what we might call a verbal tic. He would repeat a word over and over and over, sometimes for as long as an hour. During the year or two he was with me he would use my name to calm himself. So suddenly I would hear it begin from across the room—"Mrs. B, Mrs. B, Mrs. B...." When I would look at him he would give me a nervous smile but he was unable to stop himself. We had an agreement. I kept a desk in the far corner of the room and whenever he began his chant, he would be asked to go sit in the desk so the rest of us could work in relative peace. When the need abated, and he was settled, he could simply return on his own initiative. So we sometimes conducted class with the background hum of "Mrs. B, Mrs. B, Mrs. B...." I was very fond of Jay and I hope the world has been kind to him over the years.

Trina was a little chunk of a girl. She had a mighty feisty spirit that you had to admire. And oh, was she stubborn. More than once when the recess bell rang, she would decide she was not ready to end her playtime. Eleven or twelve other special needs students do not wait patiently in a line for very long, so we had little time for her antics. I knew that she was fed by both negative or positive attention from teachers or children, so I would turn and give noticeable attention to the other students waiting in line, while reaching behind me and picking up the little Trina, and carry her squirming under my arm to the classroom all the while giving her no eye contact. (My back was strong in those days.) At the classroom door I would deposit her gently still without any words or eye contact, and she would smooth down her shirt and shorts (school uniform), and walk nicely through the door, and on with the day.

Trina had a behavior specialist who worked with us. I liked this woman. She got down and gritty with Trina. One day Trina gave her a hard head butt right into the woman's pregnant belly. Fortunately there was no damage done. I was not as impressed with most of the behaviorists who came through my classroom. Many were right out of university with no classroom experience. They spent hours and hours observing, taking data, enough data to write a thirty to forty page report. I always read the report, after all they worked so hard to gather the information and the incidence data was interesting to me, but rarely were their behavior programs usable in my classroom, not with twelve to fourteen special needs students to teach.

I am resisting giving any advice on how I addressed any or all behaviors of my students, because the list is very long, and as varied as the students themselves. Although all of the detrimental behaviors in the stories I tell in this book did lessen if not completely disappear over time, certainly I had no corner on successful strategies. This is not a How To book, but I found that How To Start was by first observing each child with respect, and then consider the what and when of a behavior, and whether it interfered with social interaction or learning. Then, I found out what motivated each student. And I took it from there.

My students liked routine and it helped them stay calm and feel their world had some solid foundation when they could count on a schedule. But alas, they also lived in world where things are always changing. Flexibility is a very important trait for all children to learn and I tried to help my students adjust to changes that would inevitably crop up no matter how predictable I tried to make their school day. And of course I entered each school day knowing that the unexpected would happen. It might be something severe like a little boy having a grand mal seizure, or an upset parent coming to pay a visit at a busy time of day, or a student melting down and being aggressive.

Sadly, it could be a child showing up with bruise marks and an innocent comment about her father shaking her. This of course necessitated a call to Child Protective Services. I had a policy when this happened to call the parents after I called CPS and after I told my principal. Sometimes the parents were very angry at me but I would explain that I was mandated by law to report these things, that I cared about their child, and that they could expect a visit from CPS. It was hard to make those calls but I felt it was very important not to be an anonymous reporter but to be the face of their child's advocate to the parents. This never back-fired on me, but remember, I had already spent great energy building bonds of trust with my student's parents. When I had to report families to CPS it felt important that I be straight up with them and tell them, and remind them that we all wanted what was best for their child. Yet I won't advise this strategy to a new teacher. It should be discussed with administration first.

Expecting the unexpected was sometimes not a serious matter but just a small opportunity to be taught a lesson by a child. One situation comes to mind. A new student came, a beautiful little girl who seemed to fit in alright. But the first day soon before lunch time she taught me a big lesson. My classroom had learning stations, and the children would rotate from station to station giving them opportunities for learning to work independently, and also opportunities for me to have one-on-one teaching time or small group time. One independent station was a puzzle station. I am very fond of puzzles myself and for the students I provided many of varying degrees of difficulty. On this day all was quiet in the room. Too quiet. I should have been suspicious. I was busy working on reading with two children, my aide was doing some math with two others. When it was time for lunch I looked over to where the new girl had kept herself occupied for fifteen minutes, in my puzzle corner.

Somehow I swallowed the exclamation that came to my mouth. She had quietly and very efficiently dumped out every puzzle in the corner onto the floor. The pile of puzzle pieces was up to her knees and surrounded her like a large puddle. She smiled at me. I stared, but didn't know what to say.

My aide took the students to lunch. I spent my entire lunchtime on the floor in the corner putting the puzzles back together again. While I sat there I thought about what this child was trying to tell me. Perhaps it was simply too much stimulation or too many choices for her. Or maybe she had pulled out a puzzle, tried, but could not put it together, so in frustration had tried another and then another until the game became to dump every puzzle on the floor. Another child might have done this with great fanfare and shouts. I would have noticed sooner. Not this one. I quickly devised another system for the puzzle corner where students had a color coded box of puzzles that was appropriate to their ability level. This worked very well.

One tiny lesson taught from one little girl. Multiply this by hundreds of lessons in the course of a week. Eventually even the densest of us teachers catch on, if we are paying attention.

Sixteen

Use the Village

Ask any kid. Bathrooms play a big role in school life, unfortunately also in the life of bullies. Bullying can happen anywhere on campus but bathrooms are the preferred location for most bullies who are generally cowards at heart. No matter how watchful "Yard Duty" can be it is hard to be everywhere at once and a bully knows this. Bathrooms provide a great spot to corner a special needs child or any child who seems vulnerable.

But my classroom was in good proximity to cut off some of the potentially dangerous behavior; in the two locations I nested in at my school, I was next to the bathrooms both times. Sometimes it was very noisy, but if I was in my classroom at recess I often heard and was able to intervene for not just my student's safety but others as well. I do recall one satisfying encounter. Some girls were loudly talking and laughing in the bathroom one day, not a bullying situation this time, just upper grade recess shenanigans while I was trying to have a reasonably calm classroom for my lower grade students. So I left my classroom with my aide in charge and walked the few feet to the bathroom door.

I stood in the doorway and the girls grew silent. All I had to do was slowly and meaningfully drawl out, "Girls, I can hear every single word you are saying." I let that sink in and with a dramatic flair departed. They slunk out of the bathroom and I never had a problem with that bunch again.

Like all teachers, I had recess duty on a regular schedule, but not every day, and my aide had a well-earned break at that time, so my students were initially on their own at recess. The other teachers had varying degrees of understanding about my students. Some were very empathetic and skilled themselves at dealing with unusual behaviors, others were insensitive and judgmental, making sure I knew that in their opinion, "those children" should not be on a public school campus. Fortunately that breed of teacher was in the minority even when I started my public school career and soon faded into retirement. Still, most often the teachers came to me for help when my students had an issue.

And in time as my caseload became tilted towards children with more extreme challenges, the district finally hired a half day aide to help me cover recess and lunch time and some toilet duties. What a blessing she was. I'll call her Peggy. She was in excellent physical shape and could outrun any of my students, no small feat, and had a temperament of firmness mixed with joy and love for the students. She brought fun and more laughter into our classroom, and also carried out an important tenant of my teaching philosophy, that we Special Education teachers were ambassadors and personal relations advocates (PR) for our students and for all people with special needs. Like I always tried to do, in the lunchroom and on the playground, Peggy reached out to the general education students of the school and helped build bridges to our students.

When I was on playground duty or if I heard of an incident of name calling or bullying, I would always find the perpetrator and engage them in conversation. Occasionally I found a child who was so mean that they were unrepentant and I would sadly conclude that he or she might spend the rest of his or her life being mean and ugly to others. But for the most part, the students were not intending to be cruel. And by helping them understand my students, letting them help, getting the kids together, they often became the strongest ally any Special Education student would have. I would see these children who had been laughing at and calling my students "retard" or worse, now getting after other children who were taunting or teasing my students. And some of these former name callers became my classroom helpers.

Our school was a K - 6th grade school. Those sixth graders were ready to move on and needed activities and challenges to occupy their school days. I gave workshops in their classrooms to teach disability awareness and, from these classes, regularly recruited helpers for my classroom. I had numerous students who would gladly give up their noon and morning recesses to come and help. In fact, I had to limit the number, and I found the ones who would be most helpful to me and encouraged them, and I also took on a few of the students who really needed to be taught how to be helpful as well.

One day these 6th grade helpers proved their worth to me. On a horrible day, October 17, 1989, my wonderful classroom aide, I will call Vickie, collapsed on the floor of my classroom. (I remember the date precisely because a few hours later on that same day the Loma Prieta earthquake shook San Francisco and Santa Cruz causing massive damage.) Our classrooms had no outside telephone. And we had no cell phones then. All we had was an intercom to the office. Fortunately Vickie was on the floor right near that phone so I could be close to her while in communication to the office manager who was in turn on the phone to the paramedics.

Another huge piece of good fortune is that at that moment two of my most amazing 6th grade helpers were with me on their lunch time. They had helped me out all year long and were naturals I am sure they are in leadership somewhere today. As I saw Vickie turn gray and then collapse, I turned to the two twelve year olds and told them to take my children next door to the competent and unflustered first grade teacher and to whisper to her what had happened. I asked the girls to stay with my students until I excused them and not to worry about their own teacher, that I would take care of it.

Those two self-possessed young ladies gathered up my twelve students who were either ignoring the catastrophe before their eyes or coping with it using various behaviors that might be described as "freaking out"—spinning, rocking, crying, speaking very fast, curling up in a ball, and so forth. Getting those unnerved children to line up and move out the door in a remarkably speedy but calm manner was the best gift I could have had at that moment. The helpers then stayed next door, taking care of the students for the next hour until all had calmed down in our classroom. Their efficient action let me attend to Vickie, support her as instructed by the paramedics via our office manager, until the ambulance arrived and took her to the hospital. Vickie's condition was very serious for some time and she did not return to work for months.

I was very fortunate to have had a series of high quality helpers and volunteers through the years. I developed an especially close bond with my support staff, my assistants. Their solid back-up was a pragmatic necessity. How many times did I have to run out the door to take care of a issue, needing the competent and knowledgeable aide to be In Charge for a moment or ten until I was back. Or sometimes, I would send my aide out the door on a mission of mercy. And when I was absent and a substitute spent the day with my class family, I felt it was very unfair that the substitute got the teacher pay when indeed it was my aide who was running the classroom, keeping things going.

Their presence was not just practical help. My aides always provided me with companionship and partnership, helping me feel not so alone on the tough days and giving me someone with whom I could laugh, roll my eyes at the crazy moments, and rejoice when a child made progress and achieved a milestone of small or large significance. In referencing my staff assistants, I try to learn to use the word paraprofessional because it certainly reflects more respect than the word aide, but in the 1980s and 1990s we generally used the word aide. Aide is closer in the alphabet to Angel and Agile, so it still works for me.

Seventeen

We Don't Always Know Why

During my first twenty years in Special Education, I taught students who had more pervasive disabilities than those in my last fifteen years. These earlier students often had challenges that affected their functioning in a more extreme manner, in motor skills, in communication and language ability, and/or in cognitive thinking and performance domains.

Sometimes the etiology of a child's disability was clear. The child might have experienced loss of oxygen during the birth process and now presented with symptoms categorized as cerebral palsy. Some babies were changed prenatally by maternal drug abuse. A typically functioning baby might have had the misfortune to develop a high fever due to encephalitis or some other illness and suffered brain damage and seizure disorder afterwards. Or a head trauma might have led to a physical or cognitive handicap. These are bitter experiences to parents and they can be tormented with thoughts of, "what if" or "if only" or "what could I have done to prevent this incident." But at least they have a clear cut explanation, and just as with an adult who suffers a terrible accident or illness that leaves them impaired, ultimately parents and children do need to move forward to make a positive experience out of the new reality. I have always been moved by the courage of these families, but as they would tell me, what else could we do?

There is another group of disabling conditions with less clear causes that still fall into recognizable groups, sometimes identified in a laboratory or by physical or behavioral characteristics. For those who specialize in genetic medicine or work in the field of special education it is known that many syndromes and conditions fall into these categories. In relation to the whole human spectrum, the incidence of these syndromes is small, and the average person would only be aware of a genetic disorder that might be present in someone in his or her family or neighborhood.

Naturally there are questions and anguished self-examinations that come up in the case of a syndrome diagnosis as well as in the traumatically caused disability. A parent may entertain questions about his own genetic history, perhaps even feel a sense of inferiority in his or her genetic pool, or a sense of blaming one side of the family for an inherited genetic code. There may be a sense of guilt for not knowing about a genetic possibility, for not getting genetic counseling. Grief and shock can take many forms. We humans are pretty good at beating ourselves up, and/or also for placing blame on others in order to protect ourselves. In the end, neither of these inclinations are helpful, although there is merit in examining the ugly feelings when they do rise up in our sorrow. Special care is needed to make sure families stay compassionate and rational at these times. In the end, however, at least the families who have a child with a syndrome or identifiable disabling condition receive a concrete explanation for the challenges and differences their child faces. These explanations are also helpful for the child when they grow up and want answers for their own questions.

But sometimes, there is no clear explanation for why a child is motor challenged, cognitively impaired, or has enormous difficulty with speech and language or social skills. And frankly, "this just plain sucks" (as one parent told me). The symptoms are there. The evidence is clear. The daily life of the child is impacted mightily. The child is not functioning within the normal expectations for a child of his or her age, and it is making life challenging, maybe even downright miserable. And yet sometimes no one, from a highly trained specialist to a psychic can give a satisfactory explanation as to *why*. This is often the hardest dilemma for a family to face. To deal every day with a beloved child who struggles to learn, move and play, to speak and understand language, and make friends, who is often not accepted by other children or adults and to not know why, this is heart breaking. We humans like to have answers. We like things to be concrete. Perhaps we just need to know, or maybe it is easier to think we can fix things if we know why.

I deeply sympathize with parents who search for answers, sometimes going to specialist after specialist looking for an answer to their *why*, if not also a solution to fix things. At times, answers are found, steps are taken, or families at least gain a little more understanding of the source of their child's difficulties. Some solutions work for one child but not another. And unfortunately sometimes family's vulnerable needs are blatantly manipulated by opportunists or well-meaning programs, causing parents to get hopes high, and spend a great deal of time and money, only to be crushed by disappointment despite all their efforts paid for by their precious resources. These gurus and programs may be desperately grasping for straws themselves, be misguided and self-absorbed, or in fact may be unscrupulous and exploitive.

But, would I discourage a parent from pursuing answers? Never, because many of the discoveries that have helped us progress in the development of special education treatment - techniques, programs, therapies, and medical advances - have come about because of the unfailing love-driven research and activism of parents. My observation, though, is that my wisest parents have learned that while they keep pushing for answers, they must also accept what is, even when they do not have answers, because otherwise their life and their child's will pass by far too fast, full of bitterness and unresolved emotions. *The lesson is not to give up searching, but to enjoy life in the meantime because the child you have is the child you have, on this day today.* Our children need the parent to be present with them each day, not solely caught up in pursuit of an explanation or cure that may never happen. Nor does the child benefit from a parent filled with anger at the inexplicable injustice of the disability.

Through the years I have seen parents represent the best and sadly the worst side of this lesson. How well we understand this lesson makes a difference in the quality of this short life we all have. I came to believe that somewhere between accepting without question what we have been given, and having an unrelenting commitment to pursuing answers, lies the key to a fruitful life, no matter what level of challenges a family experiences.

I believe that these issues are also very real and true for all families, regardless of the degree of the learning and physical and social challenges. Furthermore, all of us can identify some aspect of our makeup that creates an impairment in our emotional or physical functioning, so I believe that these lessons I have learned in Special Education are not exclusively for a family with a child labeled with special needs. Rather these lessons are for all of us.

Eighteen
Family Likeness Trumps Diagnosis

Little Lucinda was floppy, double jointed, and could wrap herself up like a pretzel. She had a smile to light up the hardest heart, and she was born without fingers on one hand. The baby of a large family, she was loved and spoiled by her siblings and parents, a little ray of sunshine.

Randall looked like a little man even as a toddler, solid and reliable. He didn't laugh easily but had a good belly laugh when something tickled his funny bone.

Sandra was a delicate child, with enormous brown eyes, and a fleeting but beautiful smile who had leukemia and died when she was three years old.

Joshua was a hearty, happy, curious baby, with three older siblings who doted on him. He was part of a busy, intelligent family who included him in everything, and he was strong and healthy.

Another Joshua I taught was short and blond, with glasses perpetually falling down his stubby nose. He had an endearing way of looking up at you while trying to balance those glasses on his face. He liked school a lot, and was learning to read and do math.

Trina at age six had a body as solid as a rock, short and stocky, a stubborn temperament to match, and a good sense of humor if quite self-centered. Her nose was often runny.

Clark was freckled and red haired, perfectly combed and well dressed. He had good manners and liked to laugh, which brightened his second grade classroom. He had a heart defect, but so far had remained healthy enough for school and play.

Markus was a big boy, looking quite out of place in his first grade classroom. He had his pleasant moments, but was often so obstinate and oppositional that his daily school life and home life were compromised.

All of these children, and many others I have not mentioned, had the genetic make up of Down syndrome. But their identity was not Down syndrome. While they shared some of the physical characteristics common to this syndrome in their eyes, nose, mouth, tongue, and hands, they were all different in personality and appearance beyond these few features that would label them with Down syndrome. While some of these students had health-related issues that are more common in children with Down syndrome, many of these children were very healthy. Some of these children struggled with learning to read and do math, and some were not able to use language as well as others, but all were capable of learning some level of academic and practical skills, and many of these children possessed an amazing intelligence for emotions and human understanding.

Family Likeness Trumps Diagnosis

As I was given the privilege of having children with Down syndrome in my caseload and classes over the years, I learned that despite some similar characteristics and chromosomal diagnoses, these children were much more like their families than like their diagnosis. It wasn't just the individual environment and upbringing that made a difference for each one, although that certainly played a role as for any child, but the children resembled their own birth families in hair coloring, body size, personality, likes and dislikes. I appreciated this recognition, because sometimes parents felt that the medical world and the education world took away their child, and left them with Down syndrome. So when I came to see the individuality of each student, I could help the parents be able to proudly see their child as *their* child who happened to be diagnosed with Down syndrome, a subtle but vitally important distinction.

A diagnosis is only important if it helps to explain, understand, and provide good treatment. This is true for an adult receiving a health diagnosis, or a parent receiving a diagnosis for his or her child's learning or language challenges. The diagnosis is not the person. Linda Brown has cancer, but she is still Linda Brown, and she must not become Cancer. Mr. Smith with Parkinson's, is still Mr. Smith, not Parkinson's. The child with an interesting chromosome is still Lucinda and is not now named Down syndrome.

When I left the early intervention programs and the Special Day Class room, I never worked with another child with Down syndrome; however, as a Resource Specialist, I continued to work with students with autism and Asperger's. As parents and teachers tried to learn more about how to effectively teach and parent the increasing numbers of children given this diagnosis, I saw some professionals and parents focus primarily on the cluster of symptoms that needed treatment. I sometimes saw the same tendency to label all these students not just *with* their diagnosis, but *as* their diagnosis. True, the cluster of behaviors were often similar from one child with autism or Asperger's to another, but they were never identical, and even when "similar," were not manifested in the same way or to the same degree.

Without a genetic test to decide diagnosis, such as is possible with Down syndrome, Asperger's and autism diagnoses are dependent upon the fine skills of a good diagnostician, skilled in diagnosis of symptoms but also one who sees the whole child. It also takes a diagnostician and teachers who possess the capacity to help parents and teachers see and appreciate the individual characteristics and personality of these same children. I was fortunate to work with such professionals. And of course some parents don't need a professional to make this distinction for them, but it helps to have this clear attitude on the part of the professionals in a family's life.

Just as a child with autism resembles his or her family in physical appearance, I also saw how unique each child was in personality, values, manners, and mannerisms. Both due to family genetics and home training and environment, every child was unique and belonged first and foremost to their own family. We are not our diagnoses, we are individuals, and I believe we are more like our families than like any category of diagnosis.

Nineteen

A Good Boss Can Set the Stage for Camelot

Inevitably in every occupation we will eventually encounter a poor administrator. Sometimes one is left battered and abused by this experience, and other times, it is merely wearing to go to work day in and day out without inspiring leadership. But whether your situation with a poor administrator is extreme or mild, it takes a toll.

I have had some fantastic directors and principals in my thirty-eight working years, and am grateful for their leadership, their faith in me, their humor and wisdom. I trust I never took them for granted and let them know how much I valued their leadership skills.

But there were other bosses who did not earn my respect. One principal was a nicely dressed man, smooth and a slick talker. In all fairness, had he been my neighbor I probably would have enjoyed chatting across the hedge. But he had a temper, I discovered one day. Early in my public school teaching, I sent a boy to the office because of some misbehavior in my classroom. I was relatively new to the school, and may have felt it was something that needed a principal's guidance, or at least that the child needed a time-out sitting outside the principal's office. I do not remember the offense or offenses that caused me to make this decision, but down to the office Jerry went.

Only later did I hear what had happened but first the weekend came and went. Early Monday morning as I arrived at my classroom door, Jerry and his mother were waiting for me. "Look," she called out to me, and she proceeded to pull her son's pants down to show me dark black and blue marks on his bottom. I was shocked. She knew it had been the principal who had afflicted these marks, because Jerry had told his mother, and she was furious. I was very upset. At this time, paddling was still allowed in schools. You could opt out of corporal punishment if you signed a paper to that effect. Jerry's mom had not done so, probably not thinking she would ever need to do so.

I went with her to the office and turned her over to the principal, but I knew in that moment that I would never again send a student of mine to the office unless I had a very clear understanding of what would happen if I did. From that moment on, I resolved that I would find a way to deal with all but the most destructive student behavior.

Not surprisingly, the principal used his silver tongue to come out of the encounter with no ramifications. The mother was not a sophisticated woman, and she left after signing a No Paddling letter, either mollified or feeling helpless in the presence of the authority of the principal. Later in the week, I heard from an office staff person what had happened: the principal had let the boy get his goat. The situation escalated so that his paddling became more like a beating, and as the child yelled more and more, the principal saw it as defiance and yelled back at him, with more paddling. The office person finally interrupted the loud encounter with a distracting knock on the door and a question, and the power struggle was ended.

Even as a new teacher, I knew that this was wrong, but because the principal had the legal right to paddle the boy, I never knew what else to do after that day except not trust him, and take care of all future discipline issues myself. It was a few years later that the Child Protective Services began coming into the schools to talk to teachers about what kind of observations to report. By this time, corporal punishment was gone from the schools, and that principal had retired, but the immediate lesson I learned is that I would take care of behavioral situations myself in the future. However very soon I would learn a follow-up lesson: asking for and receiving the right help is sometimes imperative.

At the opposite end of the scale, I had another principal who would not lift a finger or take any action to help me. I was by this point dealing with some very difficult student behaviors in my Special Day Classes. I was working with children who would go out of control at unpredictable times and places, doing some serious damage to themselves, other students, the classroom environment, and me. I was pretty strong, pretty tough, and knew how to prevent or diffuse most outbursts, but I took my share of scratches, spits, punches, and even bites. Occasionally, I had a behavioral therapist on board for an hour a week to help me, but for the most part, I was on my own.

This principal liked to play the organ at full volume in the cafeteria to "entertain" the student body. This was something he would do especially on rainy days. Imagine this: a cold rainy day with a crowded cafeteria of children who have not been able to go out and play all day long, and while they are noisily eating, there is an organ playing as loud as possibly as if in a roller rink. It revved up all the students, but for my Special Needs students, it was excruciating. I often would have the students come eat their lunches in my room. I had students who needed to be held tight to shut out the external noise. The principal had seemingly no idea about children and how they would react to this added noise and stimulation. He was also not very approachable so I was never able to successfully explain this phenomena to him

During this time period, I had the most difficult student ever, before or after. His name was Carl. For years afterward, just hearing that name in any place or context, would give me the shakes. In the six months he was in my classroom, I used to sit up in bed in the middle of the night, crying out, "What am I going to do?" I really didn't know. I had tried everything I could think of to help his social and language skills develop so he wouldn't be so destructive, but to little or no avail. One day after he grabbed a classmate's hair and pulled a hunk out, laughing at her screams, I put him in a time-out spot while I comforted the rest of the shaken class. I had my aide take the students to lunch, while I stayed with the boy until the others had left. Later I walked him down to the lunchroom so he could pick up his lunch before going home. (His day had been reduced to half a day in hopes that he could learn to manage a half day first and later a full day). When he got to the cafeteria, with a gleam in his eye, he knocked every lunch from the counter-top onto the floor, right in the view of my principal.

Who did...nothing. I do remember his words: "Now, now Carl." I was ready to scream myself. I didn't, but I picked the boy up and carried him out to his waiting bus, walking right past my principal who ignored me, while the boy was kicking me, scratching me, and trying to bite me. Finally, our custodian saw me struggling and came over to help me carry the boy to the bus.

I needed some serious help from someone to know what to do with this child. It was my first experience at being totally at a loss. I got no help from my principal. In retrospect, he probably didn't have a clue either, but rather than step up and try to help one of his teachers as she was getting attacked by a student, as his cafeteria was left in shambles, or at least getting the district to provide some behavioral help, he did exactly nothing.

Finally, I went to the Special Education department and found a school psychologist willing to listen. I practically got on my knees begging for help. He did help me. Eventually this child ended up in an even smaller Special Day class for children with severe autism, where he had a one-on-one aide, and if he was left alone, he did not attack others. It was a sad case. His parents could not handle him, and he had gone from group home to group home, school to school. He was the only child in my career whom I felt that I did not help at all. I often had challenging students, children with complex and confusing behaviors who were negative and anti-social, where I didn't always do the right thing, but never did I feel that I had failed a child so completely. It was not a good feeling but it would have been much better if I could have had the support of my principal. We might not have been able to meet the child's needs at our school site but at least I would not have felt quite so all alone or like such a failure with Carl. I almost quit teaching during those six months because work had become a living hell. The situation had left me forgetting all the important lessons I had learned up to that point.

Lesson here: self-sufficiency is not always what is needed. Support and the help of others really does make a difference. Leadership must be pressed to support teachers and students.

Following this principal's time with us, we were all relieved to have a new energetic woman come in as our principal. Gone was our last principal's mantra of labeling most issues as "non-discussion items." Now we had a vibrant, up-to-date, courageous leader who was hands-on and enthusiastic. She also knew Special Education and was encouraging to me. She had the courage to put a non-performing teacher on strategies. (Being "placed on strategies" meant that a poorly performing teacher who had not committed an ethical or legal infraction would be monitored closely by an administrator—a very time-consuming task for the administrator. The teacher had to meet specific and measurable written goals for improving teaching performance within a specific time frame to avoid dismissal.) This particular teacher quickly retired instead of going through this process. I enjoyed this strong principal's stay with us, but it was far too short. She left before two years were up, eventually rising to the Superintendent's office. She was with us at our school, then gone in a blink, and we felt the lack of continuity.

About this time my classes became more and more defined for "special needs" children, rather than for students with only academic and language learning disabilities. My classes now were full of children with complex and pervasive needs, some without language ability, and even some who needed toileting and diapering. Making it more complicated to plan and teach, my classes also included children with academic potential, as well as delicate but refined emotional and social skills, and teaching children with this wide range of abilities was extremely complex for me. But I never had a student like Carl again, one that would leave me bereft of strategies, one so hard to like or love. So while I needed the occasional back-up of my administrators, it was all manageable after Carl departed. My classroom was now near the office, so I was able to stay on top of what was happening if I did need administrative support.

Our next principal came and stayed for many years. I personally found her supportive. While I was on reasonable working terms with this principal, many teachers were not. The complaints from other teachers were constant. Each school site had a Teacher's Union committee whose job it was to receive the usually anonymous complaints, organize them, write them up, give them to the principal once a month, meet with the principal to discuss the complaints, write down the principal's responses, and try to help pave the way for solutions for the problems. I was on this three-person committee for many years. We funneled many hot issues to our principal in an effort to find solutions and let teachers air their grievances. I hope we helped some. I certainly know it took an exorbitant amount of time. For the most part, teachers were fearful to state their complaints directly to the principal or even let their name be known because there was no sense of trust or safety among the staff.

Eventually, one grievance that received no satisfaction went directly to the Union for consideration. We as a committee attended a meeting with our union leaders, our principal and a representative of the downtown administration. It was our job to present the issue directly to our principal in the presence of all the others. It was very uncomfortable. There were two of us who had to do this. I remember thinking to myself "Well this may end my long streak of being in the good graces of our principal. Soon I will feel the knife in my back as so many others say they have." But that didn't happen. In fact, the principal asked our advice on how to deal with the situation.

It was soon after that meeting with the union when I realized that I was desperately ready to take on a different teaching role. I had been in my Special Day Class for longer than I had ever planned on staying in one classroom. I was not happy with receiving children who needed toilet training (without adequate facilities) mixed in with my students who were ready for more academic teaching. I had come to a point in my career and life where a change was overdue. An opening came up three weeks into the new school year, and I jumped at it. My principal hired me as a kindergarten teacher, even though the subsequent series of substitutes in my "abandoned" Special Day classroom caused her no end of problems. Thankfully, my former aide Peggy completed her credential and after a few months of chaos in the classroom, she took on the challenging class with great success.

And that is how I came to spend a year as a general education kindergarten teacher right in the middle of my Special Education career. It was a breath of fresh air and a great transition gift to me, and I remain grateful to my principal for making it happen. She didn't have to open that door for me. Administrators tend to not make it easy for a Special Day Class teacher to leave for a general education classroom simply because it is hard to find capable replacement Special Education teachers.

Several good lessons came to me from this experience. One is to be honest and open whenever possible with an administrator, regardless of how capable you believe them to be. Unless the administrator is a sociopath, or a ruthless political climber, it is the best practice. Work hard at your assignment so that you have the respect of your administrator. Then speak your mind clearly and honestly when you agree and when you disagree with the administrator, but do it in private if at all possible. While it rarely changes someone's stripes completely, it does make working together in the long run smoother. There is a mutual cordiality that can be very helpful. There can be a time and place to mount a public protest or take a well publicized stand, but often it is not necessary.

There was one more lesson that came out of all of this: you never know who is going to help you out. Out of a situation that was not particularly healthy, from a principal whom I never saw as inspiring and with whom I disagreed many times, I received a gift that allowed me to go forward in my career and in my life in a very beneficial way.

If you find yourself working with a great administrator, treasure the experience, for you do not know how long it will last. I have had administrators who have made my working life feel like Camelot. I have had administrators who may not have met my expectation of exceptional leadership, but were fine individuals and earned my respect day in and day out. I will end this section with a favorite administrator story.

Ben was a man of action. Administrating by Moving Around he called it, and the invention of the cell phone made this possible. He knew everyone's name: child, parent, teacher, paraprofessional. He loved new ideas. While exceptionally intelligent, he could be goofy too. (Picture a normally elegantly dressed man doing the chicken dance, or dressing like a pirate for Halloween to delight the children.) One day after school, a student was brought back into our school office by his older sister. I happened to be in the office along with a few other teachers and the office staff when the two siblings walked in, he with blood dripping down through his blond hair and on to his shirt and the floor. "My brother hurt himself in the park," his sister said.

All of us standing in the office that afternoon would have sprinted into action within a split second. But before any of us could even move, Ben was out of his office, talking in a comforting stream with the lad, washing his face and head, sopping up the blood, locating the injured spot, getting the boy to share what had happened, bringing him out of his shock, trying to see if he possibly had a concussion. I absolutely relished seeing this man in his impeccable dress shirt and tie be willing to get his hands bloody to best serve one of his students.

The best principals and directors with whom I worked over my thirty-eight years, had one thing in common, even while personalities and styles varied dramatically. They loved their students and their schools deeply and fiercely, and this sense of responsibility and compassion resonated throughout the day, whether dealing with a medical crisis or an oppositional student across the desk from them, whether on the playground, or in a classroom or after school at events. When I read of the Newtown, Connecticut principal and psychologist who did not hesitate to try to protect their students and teachers, dying in that effort, I saw the faces of the best of my bosses and colleagues throughout the years. They would have been there too without a question.

A Good Boss Can Set the Stage for Camelot

I give enormous credit to the men and women who become principals. It is a very time-demanding and all-consuming job. While there may be some who are merely climbing the political ladder, most of the principals I worked for, even those who sometimes made a mess of things, took that very difficult leadership position because they wanted to make a difference and create better schools for students. Keeping that motive in my mind has helped me work with the less effective leaders and cherish the gifted administrators.

My conclusion is that creating Camelot, that elusive quality, depends upon leadership that will encourage all individuals - teachers and staff of course, students absolutely, and parents as well - to bring their energy and ideas forward, moving towards being active participants in the life and vision of the whole school. Creating Camelot takes strong and secure leaders to first establish a safe place of respect and care, and from there motivate and enable all members of the community to be daily activists in creating and fulfilling the mission of the school community. It is not chaos, and nor is it authoritarian. It is certainly not sleep walking. It is dynamic teamwork.

Dear Mrs. B

Thank you for putting up with me when I am sad, angray or even both at the same time. I love the way you smil whin I am sad. Thank you fo being so nice.

love, Zack

Notes I have kept for many years.

Dear Mrs B.,
I'm so glad that you didn't have the swine flu Because that Would be aful. I missed You!

Another student, a fifth grader, sent me these words: "I would get pretty tired doing your job for awhile. I don't know how you do it, having a great day working with kids."

Twenty

"Twitterpated" & Serenity Now

In the Special Day Classes that I taught between 1981 and 1997, my classes began to change from teaching children with mostly academic learning disabilities to serving children with more complex and more severe global needs. I never knew what might happen on any given day. I loved my students, and in fact liked almost all of them too (liking sometimes requires more of an effort than loving!). Early on I had learned the lesson that behaviors and disruptions were not directed at me personally, and so I was able to absorb the ups and downs in moods and behaviors of my students as just part of the exciting unknown of each day. And my challenge each day resided not only in how I dealt with outbursts, melt downs, or other happenings but how I could prevent them in the future, through helping a student work through their distress towards less disruptive behavior in the days to come.

Some unexpected events were beyond anyone's control, such as a child having a seizure or other physical emergency. In such a case, calmness was a must to help all the other students and the child experiencing the medical event. And some meltdowns became almost predictable to me, such as a child with autism who reacted to loud environments by screaming and spinning; in such cases, I could try to keep him or her out of the situation, or provide a strong secure body hug because I knew it would allow the child to tolerate the situation better. Just as the child's parents learned, I too learned what situations would most likely send a child into out-of-control behavior: changes in routine, hunger, new encounters, loud noises, weather patterns such as thunder or wind, or lack of sleep.

However, even when I prepared my students for changes in the daily schedule, kept an eye on hunger needs, posted schedules and expectations, created individual feedback and reward systems, and communicated with parents, a school day often would be punctuated with unexpected and distracting events. This is true for any classroom but even more likely in a special needs classroom. Just ask the parent of a child with pronounced autism, and they will tell you of the exhaustion and the altered expectations for any given day. They will also tell you of the love and rewards of living with and raising their child! I, too, experienced the joy of learning to know my beautiful students who sometimes found it hard to make it through a school day smoothly and without some trauma.

I was often told that I was the picture of calmness and serenity in the midst of my teaching day. But it would have accomplished nothing if I was riled up over every child who dissolved into tears when having to change a work station, struck or bit me because of something churning up inside, couldn't walk down the corridor in a line without wandering away, was too excited by unexpected noise to do anything but laugh and spin, had a big seizure, tore up papers because of nervousness, rocked and repeated the same phrase over and over again to calm himself, climbed a fence on the playground, or refused to budge when the recess bell rang. If I had become noticeably agitated, what good would it do me, or the student in turmoil, or any of my other children? None.

I learned early on as a SDC teacher that I needed to not only behave calmly but to feel that way inside, at least at the moment. *I felt instinctively that the students needed to know that I was going to help them get through the episode.* As a teacher, I needed deep inside myself, a well of serenity and responsibility that would telegraph a message to the students that clearly said, "I am your teacher and I will help you. Things will be okay. I am here with you." It may appear to an observer as being "unflappable" but I think it is something much deeper.

There were only a few situations where I couldn't access that serene spot inside myself. The story of Carl mentioned earlier, was a situation where I almost lost my sanity and came precariously close to feeling that I could not go on in the teaching profession. While I was trying to figure out how to help him, my ability to teach the other students suffered greatly. I felt worthless as a teacher. In the end I could not keep calm, or figure out a workable strategy, and I came to have great difficulty liking the boy. I was at a loss, and I showed it. I did cry for help, I did admit to being distraught. I was not happy that I had to give up on him because I liked to think that I could figure out how to achieve some success with any student who was placed in my care. It was humbling to admit that I could not handle the situation. But then again, it was a good lesson for me. Pride like this is not helpful and being humbled was not a bad experience to happen to me in the big scheme of things.

Many years later, in a different place, different time, different job, I learned a most wonderful word from Principal Ben. That word was "twitterpated." While to me this word is self-explanatory, it broadly means to get flustered or upset. The situation with my former student Carl was more than being twitterpated; it was a situation where I was unable to teach and was not effective for him or my other students. It called for "Special Education 911 emergency help." It was an exception. And they happen. But for the remaining years and students, there were probably a dozen or more situations each day that could have caused me to become twitterpated. Doing so would have led to a very tense classroom, worried students, an anxiety-ridden teacher, and a short career as a Special Day Class teacher!

There are so many events in our world that are worthy of our concern and even righteous anger. There are situations within a school, or a district, that are worth caring enough about to speak up, act for or against, press the cause, and perhaps even lose some sleep over. But for the most part, whether in a Special Day class or the relative calmness of my last fifteen years as a Resource Specialist, I found that there were very few things that were worth being twitterpated about! The ups and downs of a group teaching session, a schedule snafu, a personality conflict, a teaching strategy that proves ineffective, a caseload overload...these are all just problems in need of a solution. I believe it is especially helpful to remember this mantra when working with parents whose well-earned emotions get the better of them. If our students need calmness from the teacher, certainly parents deserve it also. Being a parent myself, I understand how worries and emotions well up and sometimes come spilling out.

It is not often that a word expresses a negative state-of-being in such a wonderfully descriptive way that it actually creates a light-hearted feeling. "Twitterpated" does it for me. It loosens me up just to utter the word. Thanks Ben. (I have since learned that the word "twitterpated" may have originated with the Disney movie Bambi.)

I have had to learn to draw deep from the well of serenity. It was my job to do so. My students needed and deserved it. My goal was to save the angst and reactive emotions for appropriate situations…like baseball games or elections.

Twenty-one

New, New, New, All is New!

In 1998, David and I got married and we decided to live in the Bay Area. We picked a city in which to live based on the reputation of the school district for my sons, but also because David's office was in a nearby town at that time and his children were within an hour's drive away. So there were many practical reasons for the move to this East Bay location but it was also very appealing with a tree-lined Main Street. It was a very different city from the Central Valley city where I had lived, worked, and raised my sons. One could make both positive and negative comparisons between the two cities but let's just say they were different. Each place had its advantages.

I took a couple of months off work to settle us all in to our new town and plan our wedding. Soon I put my application in at the local school district office. My thought was that I would apply for general education teaching positions, but if there were none, I would go back into a Special Day Class. But a day after I put my application in, I was called to come and interview for a Resource Specialist (RSP) position. I had not considered this position before, but the principal who shared the interview process struck a chord with me. Once again I made a major career decision based on instincts about people, relationship always being a priority for me. Like most of the intuitive decisions in my life, this turned out to be a good one. Principal Jessie was a fine human being and a compassionate and wise principal.

A Special Day Class teacher is a Special Education teacher who teaches a smaller self-contained classroom of students who have struggled and not been successful within the general education classroom. These students may or may not spend part of their day in a general education class for academic or non-academic subjects. A Resource Specialist (commonly referred to as a RSP) is a Special Education teacher who works with students within the general education population. RSPs may work with their students in a pull-out separate classroom for a time period set by the Individual Education Plan (IEP) for each student. The RSP may work with the student within the child's general education classroom. The RSP may only supervise accommodations or modifications the student needs to succeed in school.

The students in an RSP program range in diagnosis from Developmentally Disabled to having a mild Learning Disability, or have other disabilities such as Visual impairment, Hearing impairment, or have an orthopedic handicap, Attention Deficit Hyperactive Disorder, or be on the autism spectrum, or even be diagnosed as Emotionally Disturbed. However, the students on a RSP caseload tend to be students with less pervasive or severe disabilities than students who are in a Special Day Class (SDC). Whether the student is in a RSP program or in a SDC class, the Special Education teacher is the case manager and provides teaching and consultation support, does academic assessment, coordinates IEP meetings, and coordinates the services needed for the student from other specialists such as Speech and Language Pathologists or Occupational Therapists.

In late 1998, I took a job that had been vacated for a year by an RSP on leave of absence. The first long-term substitute had not been a good fit for the job and left a trail of debris behind. What a mess. Well, why not start out in a new career direction with a mountain to climb? Let me count the ways: new husband and home, new adjustments for our children, new (and very different) city, new job title and description, new district, new Special Education Local Plan Area, new paperwork, new requirements, new grade levels, new subjects to teach, new school, new staff, new students, and new (and upset) parents. In addition, I inherited a less-than-optimum working setup: no locked file cabinet, an aide who worked only four days a week, a shared room which meant more commotion, and finally one co-worker who seemed to like to keep people off balance. It was time to embrace change and dig down deep for inner resources. Time to put into practice every lesson I had learned in the first part of my working life. I would soon learn more lessons.

Lessons like:

- Knowing when to say "I don't know, can you help me?"
- Bluffing one staff person when he tried to make me flustered, delighting in my discomfort. I looked him straight in the eye, and pushed back.

- Trusting my instinct about people and opening up my mind to learn in this new environment.
- Getting into a training program right away and earning my RSP credential even if it meant driving hundreds of miles repeatedly over several months.
- Taking some time to enjoy these students because they were really cool.
- Taking a walk during lunch time, some "walking therapy" to sooth the soul. I found myself gazing at the beautiful hills of the ridge as I walked those lunch times, and remembering this Psalm: "I will lift my eyes unto the hills from whence comes my help."

There were days when I desperately wanted and needed some help! But as the days went by, and I worked under Jessie's kind and wise eyes, I discovered teachers who recognized the large task I was undertaking and my own "newness" to it and provided some warmth, support, and levity. I realized how much I loved working with general education students who had some learning difficulties, but were a whole new population of students for me. I slowly began to decipher the paperwork and regulations of being a RSP, and finally I began to relax and enjoy myself. I decided this was my new work within special education. A new marriage, a new location, and now a new occupation were all very appropriate to this time in my life, my mid-forties. The time period during December 1998 to June 1999 was short in months but loomed huge as my turning point. The regular RSP was coming back from her leave of absence to her old position. But now with my hard-earned RSP certificate on top of my former Special Education credentials, my California multiple subject teaching credential, and my CLAD (working with students with a second language) credential, I had two other job offers in the district and picked one based solely on location nearest to my house. What a lucky choice! I will call this new school Arthur's Court, because it was quite often to resemble my elusive Camelot. Many good things were about to begin.

The lessons I learned from opening myself up to newness after many years of familiarity gave me the strength and confidence to go on to the last phase of my working career.

we leah we eat we draw
we write we say hi and
bye to people we know

You teach you share
you smile you love us
you cherish us every
day with a smile

I am lucky to have a
teacher like you I smile
every day I see you

Jordan

I was also lucky to work with such a great fifth grader.

121

Twenty-two

Be Organized! Be Flexible!

Now I embarked on the hardest working, most complex, most professional, and finally, most satisfying years of my working life. I could quibble with myself about that last part. I had many satisfying moments through the years, and certainly the years at the Early Intervention program in Indiana had been up to this point the highpoint for me. But I think I will stick with the statement. My last fourteen years of teaching were the best for several reasons.

First, I found I loved working with children who had some learning needs but were functioning within the general education classroom. In retrospect, I believe that with no careful planning for which I can take credit, my career took the best trajectory, beginning with children with profound disabilities who taught me about finding quality in life, and then moving on to the beautiful children in my Special Day classes who continued to teach me about essential skills and communication, and of course love. But now I was working with children much like my own sons who were gifted with quick thinking skills under-laid by deep understandings, and with whom I enjoyed fantastic discussions about an amazing array of topics. My students in these next years became a great source of inspiration and delight to me, and now these months and years into my retirement as I write this, I miss the daily, often surprising, and always invigorating, connections.

Second, I was ready for the challenge of the multi-faceted job. My primary focus and joy was teaching. But now I was also an organizer of schedules, of meetings, of programs. I was a case manager and a project manager, a term I had not thought of in relationship to school teaching before. I was a consultant and advocate for students every day. This new job seemed to be a good fit for me, to help the school by taking charge of many aspects of our program needs. Being a case manager meant that I was the point person for working with parents and teachers and administrators.

Which is the third reason I loved this job. I am clearly a "relationship person," and with this position as RSP, my opportunities for interpersonal connections were off the charts! Besides the obvious relationship with my students, I had many wonderful parents to meet and support. At some point during the year, I had the opportunity to work with, collaborate with, or consult with almost every teacher in the school. I learned an immense amount from this incredible staff. It was also imperative to have a good working relationship with our principal and other administrators. Here I was lucky once again. Particularly the nine years Ben was at Arthur's Court, were extremely rich years for me. Good days or rough ones, I came to work feeling that this was indeed the right place for me to be and the right work for me to be doing.

And there is at least one more reason I loved this job. The job called for ongoing flexibility. I had responsibility for my program, which allowed me to be, at least in some regards, mistress of my destiny. If things were not working out well, it was up to me to change, or keep muddling along in dissatisfaction. With every day or week, there would be a problem in need of a solution, whether major or minor, and I loved seeing what I could change or alter to make things work better. It was similar to moving furniture in one's house. If I could tweak something just a bit this way or that, or perhaps even over-throw a major component of my program and re-address it, it could take us to a new level of success, a fresh new way to look at things. I was blessed with administrators who let me manage my program with some authority, and I was also given some fine folks to work with on these projects. This ownership gave me a sense of fulfillment and respect that went a long way towards achieving job satisfaction.

I worked harder during my years as a Resource Specialist than ever before in my career. The years at Arthur's Court were incomparable to any previous job environment because of a mix of high-level professionalism, warm and personal relationships with parents and students, and informal individuality among the staff and administration of our school. I was at "The Court" between 1999 and 2012. In the midst of horrible budget cuts leaving teachers jobless and class sizes ever growing, devastating national events such as 9/11 and wars, and escalating Special Education costs, as well as compliance and legal hassles, it felt like Camelot to me. Not that there were not difficult days, and exhausting nights and weekends spent doing paperwork and revising that schedule for the fourteenth time in three months, but despite that it felt like the best work I had ever done. I was at the height of my career; never before had I been part of such a team of teachers and specialists and administrators and paraprofessionals who were making fabulous education happen for our students.

Is there a lesson in all of this? Yes. I had the sense to appreciate the good years both because they were too good not to value and because I had worked hard to get there. Everything I had learned in the earlier years contributed to making this RSP job right for me. And I hope it helped me be an asset to those I served. The chief joy of my work as an RSP, and all the earlier years too, was helping make the world a little better for my students and their parents. If I did that even some of the time, it was a life career worth all the work.

I learned that to have good organization skills and to possess flexibility as a critical personal and professional attribute were both essential for this job. Other than a love of students, appreciation for parents, and partnership with classroom teachers, nothing will make your life as a Resource Specialist more successful than to be organized and flexible.

I developed the following chart to outline the attributes that help make a successful RSP. It is important to understand the flow. Being an effective Special Educator starts with the heart and moves out from that center. The technical skills are the focus of university classes and teacher training workshops. They are absolutely necessary, however I have placed them on the outer rim of the diagram because without the core essentials, these technical skills surround a hollow shell.

Resource Specialist Attributes

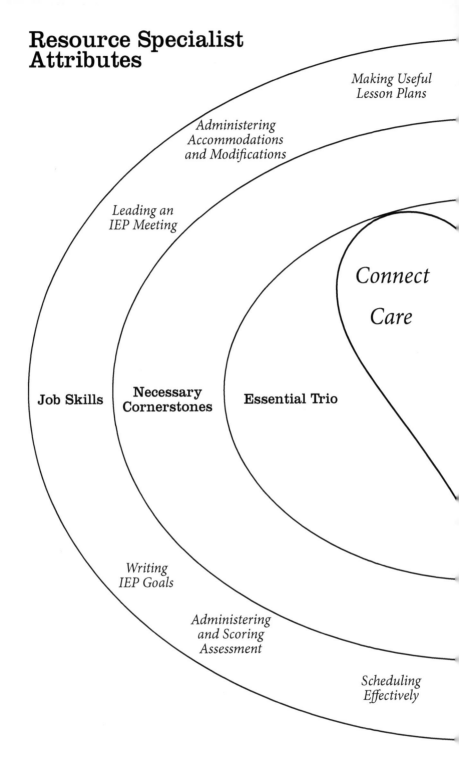

Making Useful
Lesson Plans

Administering
Accommodations
and Modifications

Leading an
IEP Meeting

Connect

Care

Job Skills

Necessary
Cornerstones

Essential Trio

Writing
IEP Goals

Administering
and Scoring
Assessment

Scheduling
Effectively

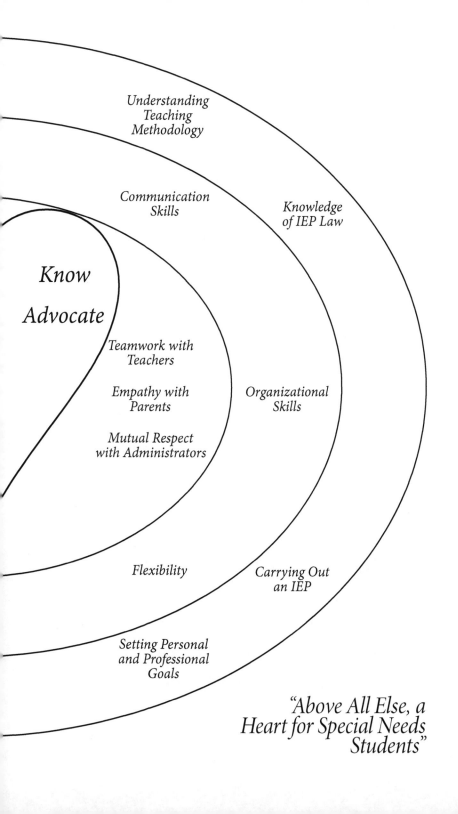

Understanding
Teaching
Methodology

Communication
Skills

Knowledge
of IEP Law

Know

Advocate

Teamwork with
Teachers

Empathy with
Parents

Organizational
Skills

Mutual Respect
with Administrators

Flexibility

Carrying Out
an IEP

Setting Personal
and Professional
Goals

"Above All Else, a
Heart for Special Needs
Students"

Dear Mrs. B,

Thankyou for helping me
with fraction and langue arts at
the begining of the school
year I didn't know how
to do fraction but I now
I'm flying through the
books.

Love,
Jessica H.

A fine artist, athlete, and a compassionate fifth grader.

Twenty-three
Faces in My Memory Window

When I think of the thirteen years I was Resource Specialist at Arthur's Court, there is no better memory than the sight of my beautiful students' faces as they appeared at my classroom door each day. Sure, occasionally I would see a sad face at the door. There was usually a good reason for that: a fight with a friend, an upset stomach, or perhaps they had had to leave a fun classroom activity to come see me and were unhappy about that. But for the most part, I saw happy faces. The joy of children, just there to be tapped so readily, never failed to move me, and also make me feel terribly responsible. I knew I must not take advantage of their openness and willingness to trust. It was my job to give them my best teaching, to make that joy of theirs go deeper and deeper into the love of learning, and to help them build a healthy feeling about their own self worth. I wanted their smiles to reflect a confidence that they were learners and that learning was exciting.

And children, like adults, need a spoonful of sugar to sweeten the discipline and hard work involved in learning to read better, do long division, spell and make complete sentences, and even stay focused. While I gave myself a strict mandate to not waste their limited time with me, I also loved the interchanges that strengthened their connections to me and to my learning environment. There is always time, if well structured, to hear about everyone's weekend. There is always time to admire a new shirt, a new haircut, a soccer victory, a birthday, a family vacation. And of course, from my standpoint as a sports fan, there was always time to talk about the latest baseball game with my student Giants and A's fans. One thing I learned is that students loved discovering a passion of their teacher because it allows them to identify something about their teacher that is humanizing. In my days in my Special Day Class, my students loved to hear about my little boys, Jack and Alex. At Arthur's Court those same little boys were grown up and hard to relate for a ten-year old, but knowing that I loved the Giants, that I loved to feed the birds, that I loved to drink tea, that I loved to go to the beach… all those pieces of information created a firm bond between my students and me, facilitating their comfort and reducing those affective barriers to learning.

It gave me rich satisfaction to look straight into the faces of my students but I also loved seeing the back of their heads as they sat industriously and enthusiastically working on their writing assignments on the row of computers I put along one wall. I liked teaching math, especially fifth-grade math where our motto was "Less Stress, More Success." Quite honestly, reading was not my favorite subject to teach, at least not learning to read. Having just seemingly learned to read by osmosis myself as a child, I found teaching reading to be a vastly perplexing mysterious process. Still, I did my best. Developing reading comprehension skills was very exciting, but my favorite subject was writing.

Reflecting my own love of writing, I found awaking the love of writing in my students tremendously satisfying. My students often thought that they hated to write, that they were terrible at writing. So to take a child with dysgraphic tendencies and get them excited about telling their stories was the best thrill I could get from teaching. "Everyone has a story to tell. Everyone can write," was a poster over my desk. It was my theme. I would help students get organized and get their thoughts on paper, then give them the computer to put their words down. In the beginning when they were young and didn't have much stamina yet, I would trade typing back and forth with them. But soon they were typing on their own, rejecting offers of help, and I would smile to see them with their heads bent slightly over the keyboard, putting their written words onto the screen. Finished pieces were edited with me, then corrections made by the student. When it was all ready, they could pick a fancy font and print it out. All finished pieces were put in a book for the end of the year. They would pick one to read to an adult guest. I don't know who had more fun with our writing: the students or me.

I have many fine notes & quotes (full of creative spelling) from my students over these years ranging from apologies ("I am sorry I was so obnoxious, I don't know how you put up with me") to good wishes ("So glad you are better. Glad you didn't have the swine flu. That would have been awful.") to thank-yous ("You rock Mrs. B" and "Thanks for making me know that I am a good writer.") But the best quote might have been by one of my fifth graders who struggled mightily with math. I had given them some pithy phrases of advice from time to time, feeling like if I used some catchy hints, it might be more easily remembered. A fourth grade girl wrote to me on the back of her homework one night, "Thanks Mrs. B. My homework wasn't so hard tonight because I used my common-sense barometer."

I loved developing a strong bond with my students, and realized that my enthusiasm could be contagious. I also wanted to work for the empowerment of my students, because I knew they would go on without me very soon. In my memory I still see their faces at my window but in fact they have all moved on. It is not important that any student specifically remembers me, but that through my work with them, something will have changed for the better within that child.

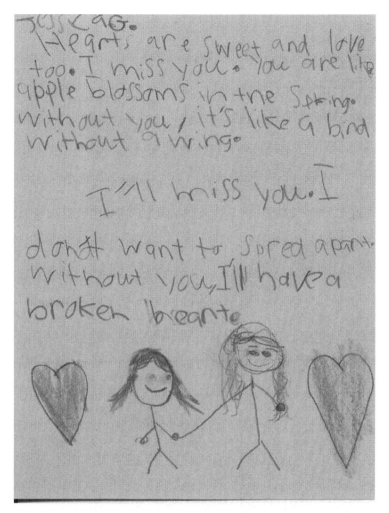

Already a deep-thinking author in fourth grade.

Twenty-four
Keeping Healthy

When your To Do list goes blank, and you have not a single Problem in Need of Solution, and your Angst Bucket is bare and echoing empty...then you had better check your pulse, because your life has ended and you have not realized that fact yet.

When I think of the most relaxing moments of my life, the most carefree minutes, hours or days, I think of being by the ocean listening to crashing waves, feeling the cool wind on my face, and sitting either in comforting solitude or in silence next to someone I love. Or perhaps I am in front of a pleasantly blazing camp fire up 8,000 feet in the mountains, with no phones and no outside interference, surrounded by a few good people who are equally content. Yet, even in those moments, if I allow myself there are things to fret about. Once we leave our infancy, or perhaps even once we leave the womb, there is no way our cares and responsibilities don't weigh on us.

But teaching these days, in American public schools, is off the charts regarding stress. Every year I taught, I saw the demands on teachers become more unrelenting. I saw teachers being drawn away from their planning and teaching into record keeping, massive assessments, and over-done accountability, all the while working with more students under more pressure from the public. Often what made this the most difficult was feeling the ugly voice of the public vilification through the news and the internet. Special Education has its own set of paperwork and compliance legalities that could threaten to turn the actual teaching into a secondary job function. In addition, many Special Education teachers worked under the threat, real or imagined, of due process and litigation possibilities.

While I joked sometimes that I hoped to finish my career without getting head lice or being sued, I was only partially joking. I did not let this thought of a lawsuit hang over me on a daily basis, but it was there in the background. I believed firmly that I should be up-front, honest, and open with my families, doing my best to both cover the legal details of any given IEP (Individual Education Plan) and establish a relationship of trust and responsibility with my families. In other words, an ounce of prevention. My Golden Rule became, "Treat your families as you would like to be treated yourself, and do your job with as much competency as you can muster." And in most cases, that is all a parent wants to see. It is what I expected and desired for my own children. The vast majority of my parents were warm, forgiving, respectful, and compassionate moms and dads, individuals with whom I loved to engage in conversation and share experiences.

However, here are at least three different ways that teachers have potential for stress.

First, there are parents who are unhappy for many reasons. They may have unresolved anger because their child has a learning challenge, and they want someone or something to fix their child, or unhappy because they interpret the law and what is actually happening with their child in a different light and with different expectations than do the professionals. And of course the parents might be unhappy because they are absolutely correct: their child is not getting the services that he or she is legally or morally entitled to receive. Discussion and mediation can help in many cases. Occasionally there is a serious disagreement and things go to court. These meetings get uncomfortable, sometimes ugly. Speaking as a person who went into education to help and serve, to teach and live in a world of learning and exploration, this kind of situation is extremely upsetting. We teachers went into the teaching field, not into law. Yes, teachers need to be accountable, and yes, some children and families have specialized and expensive needs to be met that stress a financially strapped school district. Realistically, there will be disagreements from time to time. While occasionally he or she is very responsible for the problem, most often the Special Education teacher is simply caught in the middle, and these demanding situations produce personal and professional stress for a teacher. Reflecting back, I believe that teachers could use more support and training in how to handle these time-consuming and adversarial situations with healthy detached sympathy for worried or angry parents and better problem solving skills for professional staff.

Second, another way teachers experience stress is in simply trying to complete the day-to-day work load. There are just not enough hours in the day. As a special educator, particularly as a RSP, the paperwork was daunting. I worked from 7:30 each morning through my lunch time (most days I ate a heated-up lunch at my computer while I answered email or reviewed student work). I went home after my last meeting of the afternoon hoping I had prepared well enough for the next day's teaching, and when I got home I went right down to my computer and dove into paperwork, IEP writing, and report writing, until 7:00 or even 8:00 each night when I would make myself put it away. At least half of most weekends were spent on work and preparation. And three times a year when progress reports were due, I spent probably two entire weekends on this paperwork.

The last kind of stress that comes up for all teachers - and this is the area where teachers would rather put all their time and energy - is trying to reach and teach every student in their class. I really admired how a classroom teacher could prepare and present a lesson to over thirty children who had far-ranging background information, skill levels, focusing ability, and do this when there is a potential for interruption from an announcement, or a fire drill, or a student having a disruptive problem. Whether in a smaller group in a Resource session or within a large class, I found it marvelous that good teaching could happen despite all these disruptions. But it did, every day. To accomplish this feat, most teachers worked very hard on prepping and teaching and following up. And secondly, they often worried about some students not understanding the lesson, trying to find time to re-teach the lesson for a few while keeping the bulk of the class from getting behind, as well as challenging those quick learners who might get bored. And always the State Standards hung over the teachers not merely as the guidance that they should be but as the threat of what needs to be covered before testing in May. Throw into the mix a student with challenging behaviors, serious home turmoil, or worries about playground bullying, and you have a very complex situation that most people would find daunting, if not impossible.

I could talk about stress all day long, but what lessons did I learn to deal with its intensity and to alleviate the level of stress in my life? Here are a few things that helped me:

• I took a daily walk without fail between 6:50 and 7:25 each morning, rain or shine, by myself in the neighborhood around my school. I called it a walking meditation. The air was crisp and clear, and it was dark much of the year when I started my walk. I hated getting up early, but I found it soothing to start my day by walking out to my car at 6:30 and hearing the owls in the dark trees of my canyon, and smelling the fresh earthy smell of trees, driving twelve miles on back roads with light traffic, and finally walking through the neighborhoods checking out how the neighbor's roses were blooming, and seeing the mist rise from the park in the winter. Then I hit my classroom at 7:30 ready for work.

• I also spent time talking to good people each day. Maybe I only had five minutes, but I found a good person to chat with about work or personal life each day.

• I sometimes went out to a picnic table and sat in the sunshine by myself to eat lunch away from my desk. Feeling the sun on my back and hearing the happy sound of children on the playground helped me stop the world when I needed it to quit whirling for at least ten minutes.

• When the students were in my room, I focused entirely on them. No other worries were allowed to enter my mind when children were present. Making this priority kept me certain why I was doing this work. It assured the kids that they were getting my undivided attention as well.

- Although I came home and did hours of paperwork, I put my work space in the best location I could find in my home, right by the windows overlooking my back deck and the trees of the canyon. Rather than being too much of a distraction, this allowed me to take short mini-breaks to glance up to see what particular bird was landing on the bird feeder, or how my lemon tree was faring, while the evening light (unless it was deep winter) streamed in the window onto my face. I liked working at home because I felt a sense of liberation, like I was working on my own time, away from the ever-present bells and periods that dictated school life.

- Every month or so I would treat myself to a full body massage, and float away in the silence, soft music, and skillful and soothing hands of Donna. When I reluctantly sat up from her table, I felt like a rejuvenated soul and body.

- Every evening without fail, my David and I would put work behind us and set the table, light the candles, open a bottle of wine, and put on some music. Then David would bring out whatever meal he had put together (I did help sometimes) and we would sit and enjoy our food and conversation. We would talk and share our days and experiences, and plan for something fun on our next vacation. We talked of our own children and books we had read. What a splendid way to let the day's problems and intensity melt away for the night. When David was out of town, I still sat the table to eat, and still lit a candle. I would always read while eating. This worked well to take me to a different "place," although one time I was reading so intently that my book caught on fire, being too close to the candle.

- I always found that I could deal with stress best if I had some sense of control over my time and decisions. So I would plan ahead, and set up my working time. I didn't mind working hard, and fully expected to do so, but I always felt less stressed if I could tell myself that this weekend I will do my school work on Saturday morning, or Sunday afternoon, and the rest of the weekend I will stay free to do the other activities of my life. I tried to work ahead, and work smart.

I would wish for every teacher to reduce stress by first focusing undivided attention on the students themselves, and second, strive to not get behind on required but unpleasant tasks, and then third, make time for non-job-related activities, whether exercise, games, immersing in one's own children's lives, reading, music, or travel, or whatever works best for each individual teacher. My observation is that teachers are very good at extra-curricular activities, are lifelong learners, and have an interest about the world that is unending. This vitality and open minded curiosity is the best gift teachers can give their students if they aren't too over-stressed to do so.

Twenty-five
On The Home Front

Having done me the favor of reading the preceding chapter about ways I dealt with stress in my working life, a young mother sent me a wry comment. She observed that ending my working day whenever my work was finished regardless of how late in the evening, and then sitting down to a candlelit meal, two adults talking for hours over a glass of wine, was all well and good, but not something she could relate to in her current life with small children. She asked me, "How did you combine working with raising young children?" I immediately reread my last chapter and understood her point. My stress reducers were largely geared to an empty nester or for a teacher in a pre-parenting stage of life. Yet I worked before, during, and after raising my children. How did I do it? No, that is not the question. Not how did I survive it, but was I able to make life a positive experience in the midst of raising little ones and working a demanding job? My reader deserved a response and I am grateful for the wakeup call.

First, a note. This book is a memoir of a working career. It is not a personal memoir of my life or my family. Inevitably bits and pieces of my family life have entered into my writing. Perhaps it makes it a little more interesting and also often directly pertains to aspects of my work. This particular chapter focuses on the connection between teaching and being a parent. The joyful experience of raising children adds a layer of complexity and crucial time involvement to any family's life. How did I handle my parenting in regards to my work life? What lessons did I learn? That is what I wish to address. I have deliberately minimized references to my relationship life in this chapter and throughout this memoir out of respect for privacy and due to the limited relevance to my topic.

Creating a Family Team

Passing time can soften the memory of those demanding child-rearing years into a nostalgic vision, brought about by re-visiting family photos of cute boys playing happily and creatively. This charming memory also is reinforced by seeing the fine young men who grew up from those little boys we raised.

But, of course, it was not easy. It was often messy, chaotic, exhausting, and very disruptive to any notion of a smooth flow of life. I certainly felt torn in different directions at times between work and home. Yet I can tell you, even pushing aside the sentimental curtain of the years, I have no regrets to any important degree. I can tell you that we did not do everything right, but we did make it work, that we did have many contented moments.

While sometimes we fell into bed in utter fatigue doubting and questioning ourselves, on other nights we fell asleep at the end of the day satisfied with our life. And with the blessing of the power of forgiveness (of myself and forgiveness from my children) I am happy with how we merged our working lives with raising two young boys. And I am saying "we," because it was a team, all four of us, my former husband, myself, and our two sons.

For my part, thanks to an idea from an otherwise forgotten article I read during that time period, I gave myself permission to be a "Good Enough" Mother, not a Perfect Mother, and by doing so, allowed forgiveness, and a creative spirit to arise in our family. This moved us forward using the mistakes and frustrations of the bad days along with all the laughter and cooperation of the good times, to build stronger individuals who, with time, possessed more capacity to be flexible. Boys grew into men who had perseverance enough to face a variety of challenging situations that life has since thrown at them.

We were a family team, and that is the most important stress reducer I would offer young working families. Early on, the boys learned that Mommy and Daddy's jobs were very important. For starters, we all had to work together to make sure that none of us were late for work. That meant that each morning, while it was not easy for everyone to get up and ready for work and day care, the boys soon learned not to whine and complain much, to get up, get breakfast, and get out the door by 7:00 each morning. Yes there were some tantrums, or drama about what to wear and more, but for the most part it didn't take the boys too much maturity to buy into the notion, the reality, that this is what our family did each morning and they played a role in making it work for our family.

Some organizational groundwork helped of course, deciding what to wear and laying it out the night before, packing the backpacks the night before, preparing lunches the night before, and streamlining breakfast preparation to a minimum and still meeting nutritional basics. We had to work together like a team in the morning. It was essential. But the mornings could not be without the personal element. Emotionally, one son needed a ten minute cuddle when he was preschool age. The other thrived when he had company at the breakfast table to eat his cereal. These were by necessity short interludes, but this time and attention was well worth building into our morning. Their father said goodbye to them, carrying or walking them to my car, giving them a goodbye kiss and tucking in a lap blanket around them on the cold Central Valley winter mornings. These were small psychological niceties that went a long way toward reducing the stress of a hasty morning routine.

By contrast, we all loved our weekend and vacation mornings, sleeping in, watching cartoons, staying in pajamas, and taking a long time to do anything and everything. We relished the variance in our schedule and somehow even at an early age, the boys understood the yin and yang between work/school days and home/vacation days. They certainly developed a work ethic at a young age, but they also quickly recognized how much we could enjoy the alternate side of life—play!

About the time the boys were old enough to walk, I realized that we should nix our habit of eating in the front of the television or curled up with a book. We instigated a dinner time routine. Every night we would sit down at the table. Everyone would offer a prayer of sorts; we gave a thank you for whatever had happened that day. We would hold hands for just those few minutes and be united as a family for that tiny bit of time. By each person getting a time to talk about their day, the rest of us could listen and learn. And particularly when the boys were off to school, but even when they went to day care because it resembled school, they had an understanding of what "school" was. So Dad went off to teach Adult school, and Mom went off to her school to teach a classroom different yet similar to their own school experience. All were important and we all could visualize at least to a degree what our various worlds were like.

Buy-in is a huge part of cooperation. It didn't stop a kid from being a kid; when they were not unbelievably sweet and sincere and wise, they could be out of control, upset, cranky, self-willed, and more. Children are not little adults. And absolutely if you have a child with special needs, the time and patience needed by the parent may be magnified by many degrees. But by developing buy-in, it helped our boys become more reasonable about how our household ran, and taught them respect for each other and respect for our students. They also knew that sometimes their mom and dad had rough days and had problems we struggled with in our working lives. The boys would ask us about these problems the next day to see how things were working out.

And it occurs to me that these nightly dinners together as a family when the boys were young, were just a noisier, messier, more unpredictable and abbreviated version of the candlelight, wine and fine dinners I would have later with my husband David. They served the same purpose, to reduce stress by sharing time together, sharing experiences together, and to feel the love and support of the most important people in our life. They were a centering point in the whole busy time-pressured day.

It was sometimes a trick to make that evening meal happen during the school age years, when there were homework assignments, sports practices, choir practice, Scouts, church meetings and more, that competed for our valuable hours each evening. And we had four people to consider; it was simple when the boys were younger, but every year it got more complicated as the boys each developed a life of their own. We parents too had commitments at church and at work that sometimes extended into the evening hours. But for the most part, our evening dinner together was kept as a priority. The boys helped clean up afterwards, in age appropriate manner. This worked for us. Other families may have even more demands on their time, or work odd or shifting hours, and one size or style doesn't fit all. Each family needs to determine what makes things work for them to keep connections and buy-in flourishing.

One evening I was not feeling well. It was always a dilemma, and is for any teacher. Should I stay home and take care of myself or go into school? Staying home meant using a precious sick day. It meant working doubly hard to write user-friendly lesson plans for a substitute. It also meant that some degree of my teaching program would not be effectively played out that day with my absence. Still, going in to work sick was not a good idea for my own well-being or my students'. I was debating this decision when one of my sons very seriously advised me, "Mom, you should go in. Your class won't like to have a substitute. Kids don't like subs."

There is no question that with this comment, at least from his perspective, he showed his involvement with me in my working life. Overall, the boys simply accepted that I worked. It was just the way things were and they felt I played an important role in the lives of other kids.

What I learned during these busy years was that making my teaching a family affair not only reduced my stress in working and child rearing, but also taught our young children to be less self-centered and more empathetic in the short and long term. One significant caveat needs to be added. It was critically important for my own children to know and feel that they were the most important persons in the world to me, and that I would drop everything for them if they needed me, and sometimes I also dropped everything for them when they didn't really need it just because I wanted to do so. I hope they felt that.

Balancing Work Demands & Family Time

Certainly there is no question that the type of teaching I was doing when my sons were young was well suited to allow evening and weekend home time with my children. And some of this was just dumb luck, but much of it was deliberate. Shortly before my children were born, I quit working thirty miles from home where two hours of each day were spent on commuting. When the boys were born and in their growing up years, I took a new job two miles from home, and put them in day care and then in public schools that were in close proximity to my work site and our home. I used proximity to great advantage.

During these lively child rearing years I had a teaching job in the Special Day Class that was exceedingly demanding, quite physical, and unpredictable during the hours the students were present. However, while the teaching preparation and the paperwork requirements took some after teaching hours, the preparation time was minimal compared to the time I needed to give to my work years later as a Resource Specialist. And again, I had some choice in that matter. Once I became a mother I deliberately stayed with a known teaching situation instead of changing jobs every few years as I did in my twenties. Therefore, I freed more time to spend with my sons. I had long before found myself uninterested in climbing the ladder professionally so this was fine with me. Of course I did miss out on expanding into more varied teaching experiences which, without children, I would have done during those years. I made this choice knowingly and willingly because my goal was having time with my sons, while still doing a honorable and thorough job with my students. The learning curve for any new assignment is time consuming and I chose not to take those new positions during my sons' formative years. It was a career sacrifice I suppose, but I have no regrets whatsoever.

Every father and mother makes his or her choice. There is no one right answer. But I knew what course I felt was right for me. *Without a clear loss to my family and to my sanity, I could not have it All, but I could have all that was important in family and career.*

And there turned out to be plenty of time to expand my working life and take new roles later on. We all talk about how little time there is in life, and how fast time passes. That is all true, but another way to look at life is that for most of us there is more time than you might imagine. There are stages that come and go, and a real ebb and flow in life. Those job advancements or promotions, or the extra assignments or extracurricular activities will be there in years to come. Granted in some fields, job promotions may be more time sensitive. In such a situation a person might feel they have to strike while the iron is hot to get the right job. I can only speak for myself. I liked being in the trenches. It was fascinating enough for me to change those trenches from time to time, but in the years that our boys were young, I stayed in the same classroom and tried to make it an ever-growing and ever-changing environment. I wanted to make life transformations on the front line, doing the nitty-gritty work.

When many personal changes came about in my life in 1998, I found that new career opportunities were also readily available. At home, our children no longer needed the same kind of attention as when they were younger, and I was in the position to take on more time consuming challenges. As a Resource Specialist, the teaching itself was not as physically demanding as in my Special Day Class, but the new job did involve very long days with many meetings, and into the evenings and weekends too with paperwork. It was my choice not to have a job with that kind of workload when my children were small, although I observed that other Resource Specialists made it work. The important lesson for me was to be intentional about my decisions, and then carefully monitor my family's well being.

Expand Your World

Here are some other stress reducers that worked for me when I had young children. I took a year of maternity leave, and while the money was tight for a year, I didn't need to hand my little babies over to someone else to care for them. We had no grandparents available to babysit. I spent months during my maternity leave seeking the perfect day care and I found it. Finding Sharon reduced my stress dramatically.

By the time I went back to work, the boys were toddling and ready for new adventures themselves. I remember the first day back at work in 1984. About lunchtime I had the startling recognition that for the last two hours I had not once thought about my little boy. I had been too preoccupied with work. This disturbed me at first. What kind of mother was I? But then I started to understand. My little baby boy was a person in his own right. It was the real beginning of cutting the umbilical cord. True, he was now having experiences I would never know about. All day while I was at work, he was laughing and maybe crying, he was watching, learning, modeling, playing, discovering, eating and sleeping. And for those hours each weekday, I was not there to watch. With our unflappable and utterly trustworthy Sharon and all his new playmates, my son developed his own life, a separate being from me, the beginning of the rest of his life. It was a very healthy realization. Over the years, both boys brought home much to talk about at the dinner table. They were growing their wings. And their roots remained strong as well.

And in the midst of all of this rich and crazy life I led as a teacher and a mother, it helped to find even tiny ways to feed my own soul and mind. I somehow found time to play tennis and sing in the choir. And during one of the most insanely busy times in my life, when my sons were preschoolers and my classroom was filled with children with very special complex needs, I helped start a book club. It was a statement to myself that reading was not just for summer vacation. Yes, it was statement that I could indeed read at least one good work of fiction or nonfiction each month, regardless. Reading was a gateway to sanity and expanded horizons. At a time when my daily world could be seen to be composed of small details and very immediate needs, I needed an outlet to broaden my thinking, to let my imagination become free and limitless. We gathered a group of working women, many also in their child rearing days, and we met one Friday night a month. We would stumble into our gatherings, weary bleary from our working and family lives, and three hours later, after scintillating stimulating discussions about our chosen book, we would emerge refreshed, energized and ready to take on our world again!

When my days got crazy, and they often did, it was pretty important to keep my sense of humor, share tales with sympathetic friends, and very importantly develop an ability to take a step back and be the outside observer. I read somewhere that we should all have to parent (or teach) with a mirror in front of us. What does our face say to those looking at us? Wow. That was a startling thought. Visualizing how I was presenting myself to my children and to my students really put things into perspective for me. Being present to my sons each day, with a face that says I love you and am happy to see you, was very important to me. And they would tell me when they thought I looked sad or mad. Not that they shouldn't see mad and sad sometimes, but for the most part, I wanted them to see love.

Take Your Rest When and Where You Find It

I offer a final story as a humorous take on how I learned to take advantage of any moment that could be used to better take care of myself during those exhilarating and exhausting years of teaching and parenting.

It was 3:30 p.m. I sank into the reclining dental chair, still huffing from the early dash away from school to my dentist office. The smiling assistant put the bib around my neck, carefully avoiding catching my long hair in the clip. As she lowered my head down until I was horizontal she chattered in a familiar manner. We knew each other well. I was undergoing a series of crown work, and was only half way through. I was thankful for modern dentistry, and for my insurance, and for the gentle hands of my dentist. Soon, he was standing beside me, greeting me while double checking my x-rays. For the next two hours I would be in his capable hands. I sighed, closed my eyes and felt a sense of calmness come over me. I would have two hours to rest my weary ever-moving body. For two hours I did not have to be responsible for anything other than rinsing and spitting and tilting my head in the direction needed. These visits to my dentist were providing me with the most peaceful moments in my busy life of working and mothering young sons.

The dentist and his assistant laughed at me. Most of their patients dreaded the dentist's chair, especially for long procedures. Others were restless, fidgeting, and anxious to get back to their daily schedule. I, to the contrary, was exhausted, if happily exhausted, between my parenting busyness and the demands of my teaching job. Throw in my lack of sleep and a life full of constant interruptions, and I had come to a sincere appreciation for the two hours on the dental chair because I had no choice but to stay still. No one would call me, no one would interrupt, no demands needed to be met, I didn't even have to think. This enforced stillness was a gift. Not exactly like a spa, but a gift nonetheless, and by golly, there was no other choice but lie back, close my eyes, open my mouth, but not say a thing!

My Hope

What is the lesson I learned during my years of raising children and teaching? Barring an extreme crisis like ill health, no matter how sleep deprived or how chaotic my life felt, and no matter how many mistakes I was sure I was making, when I could think creatively and act compassionately, and take care of myself, I could then work towards a home life that I hoped would leave a rich legacy for my own children and still be able to serve my students with the greatest sensitivity and skill.

That is a big dream, and a big mouthful! But it was not all up to me. In truth, a happy family life could only happen when we all worked together as a family team. It was my job as a parent to foster that vision.

It may not always have looked perfect, but I hope it will be remembered that it looked like love.

Twenty-six

Something New Around the Corner

And now back to close this narrative. Why retire from such satisfying work? It was time. That is the best answer. There are details of course. There always are. The small portion of Special Education work that I always disliked but had learned to tolerate, became too distasteful, and began to feel like it was the tail wagging the dog. Compliance issues were taking more time and I felt restless, that it was time to do something new. I felt my resiliency for the stressors was ebbing and I wanted to leave while I was able to give 100% to my students and to my responsibilities. Fortunately, I am happy to say that I not only survived thirty-eight years of an admittedly stressful career, I loved my students and the teaching to the last day.

I retired in June 2012. I tied up the loose ends, and said fare-wells to students, parents, and staff. Telling my students goodbye was emotional and they each reacted as fit their personality; the children were forthright and true to themselves. Max, a little spit-fire with a golden heart spoke straight from that heart as he said quietly, "There will never be another you, Mrs. B." This gave us a wonderful opportunity to talk about how unique each one of us was, how there would never be another of any of us. In another fourth grade group, the children were almost in tears and ex-pressing their sense of loss, when bright-eyed little philosopher Elliot spoke up with pure childlike wisdom: "But we have today!" That made us all smile and realize that there was no use moaning and worrying about the next year. We had that day and the re-maining few weeks of school to relish each other.

But the most significant tribute I received was from a parent. I will take this voice of connection with me the rest of my life. She told my coworker: "When I am with C'Anna, I feel the same way I feel when I am in Yosemite. I feel that everything is going to be okay." No professional evaluation could ever match these words. I was honored and humbled. I don't ever recall feeling as solid as El Capitan, but it makes me satisfied to hear that I have in some way provided a sense of competency, comfort and strength to someone else when they needed it most. In turn, this strong and authentic parent may never realize all the life lessons I learned from her

After the school year was over, I cleared out the classroom taking remarkably little home. My memories were huge, and I didn't need many tangible reminders of a good career. I went to the beach, and there in my friend's cottage by the rocky shore, I spent two weeks reading carefully and with great love the cards and letters from staff, parents, and children. Those letters were the most incredible gift I could have received.

My best description of this momentous event of retirement is that I closed the door gently but firmly, and now is a new day, a new focus. This memoir, *Dear Mrs. B*, is part of the moving on. I believe that retrospective precedes a creative future. First this memoir, and then something new, some writing that is more creative and not so introspective.

Now as I am completing this memoir it is autumn of 2012. I feel rich because of my teaching experiences. We can hopefully all say that, regardless of what our life's work has been. Most of all, I am immensely grateful that I have had the capacity to appreciate these unplanned lessons and countless others.

And Camelot? It would be far too corny to say that I found my Camelot, and it was inside of me. But regardless, I will say it, and then laugh out loud.

Glossary of Special Education Terms

This book is not a primer on Special Education. As important as these subjects are, I was not interested in writing on teaching curriculums, Special Education legal processes, delve into definitions, or explore historical changes. Others have written of these matters. I lived and breathed teaching methodology and legal procedures every day of my working life. By contrast, *Dear Mrs. B* is about the human experience and the many lessons I learned.

At times in my working life, I struggled with the language of my field. At one time the word used most often was "handicapped," and then "disabled." Is it possible for people who have special needs to get special services that are life changing, necessary and expensive, without labels that indicate "less than?" Words that imply that there is something wrong with an individual? These are disquieting thoughts. Many now use the word "challenged" to pair with the area of life that is indeed challenging for an individual. And given that almost all of us can recognize areas of our own functioning that are "challenged," this might be, for now, the best word for conversation.

Words, labels, terms, diagnoses, eligibility requirements will continue to evolve, and may be spelled out quite differently both legally and culturally by the time you read this book. I am sure the language discussion will continue for years to come. But I can unequivocally state that regardless of words and labels, in my opinion the legal birth of Special Education has been a remarkable and positive force in the lives of millions of students across the country, even with all the flaws we humans have brought to the table in carrying out the mission.

For those unfamiliar with Special Education, here is a brief and casual glossary of Special Education terms intended solely to provide general guidance. These are not all-inclusive definitions.

Accommodations & Modifications: Many children with special needs benefit from special program accommodations and/ or modifications in order to be successful in academic or social arenas. These could include specially designed furniture for a child with a physical disability, Braille for a blind child, a special assistant for a child who has had issues with aggression, or preferred seating location for a child with attention deficit disorder, vision or hearing impairment. It could include special paper or computer use for a child with motor or writing issues, multiple bathroom breaks for a child with health needs, special buddies or check ins from the teacher for a student with emotional needs, or having test questions read aloud to a student with a reading disability.

Autism: Children diagnosed with Autism Spectrum Disorder have difficulties (sometimes extreme) with language and social communication and sensory issues. Children with Asperger's have high cognitive and verbal skills but also have poor broad based communication and social skills, and often sensory disturbances. Individuals diagnosed with ASD or Asperger's present on a spectrum from mild to extremely disabled. There is some disagreement about whether these two, ASD and Asperger's, should be included in the same category.

Communication Disabilities: Children who are diagnosed with a communication disorder by a Speech-Language Pathologist (SLP) may have significant difficulty in the areas of speech articulation (correctly producing speech sounds), speech fluency (stuttering or cluttering), or vocal pitch/quality. A student with a language disorder may have difficulty acquiring age-appropriate vocabulary, and/or have issues with word retrieval, using appropriate grammar, and sequencing, or understanding spoken or written language. The student may also exhibit difficulty understanding social cues and situations and using appropriate social skills with peers and adults.

Down syndrome: A prenatal chromosomal disorder causes the child to have varying degrees of cognitive limitations and a cluster of physical and sometimes health related symptoms. There are many genetic syndromes that cause cognitive or motor impairment, but in my working career, Down syndrome was predominant.

FAPE: The law grants all students the legal right to a Free and Appropriate Public Education. Sometimes there is disagreement between school districts and families as to how to interpret this law.

Inclusion/Mainstreaming: Children who have diagnosed special needs may spend part or all of their school day within a general education class. Sometimes these students have an aide provided by the district Department of Special Education. More typically, the classroom teacher works with the guidance of a visiting Inclusion Specialist.

Individual Education Plan: The IEP is a legal document that guides all services for a student. The IEP includes goals and objectives written for every area of school in which the child is not functioning within the range of his/her peers. The IEP is written at meetings attended by parents (and possibly advocates), the classroom teacher, Special Education teacher, specialists, psychologist if appropriate, and administrator of the child's public school. IEPs are held at least annually, with Triennial IEPs held every third year to establish and verify eligibility for special education services.

Intellectual Disabilities: When an individual has low cognitive ability coupled with below average social adaptive skills, he or she may be classified with intellectual disability or cognitive impairment, or as mentally retarded. At one time, many children were diagnosed in this broad category, but with finer diagnostic advancements, more children may now be given a primary disability in the areas of autism, language impairment or other.

Learning Disability: Learning disabilities can cause learning and social endeavors to be mildly to severely impacted. They can be diagnosed in children and adults by a trained assessor using standardized and informal assessment tools. Disabilities can be found in attention, and/or in one or more areas of visual, auditory, language processing or production.

Least Restrictive Environment: The philosophy and law that states that children should be learning in the environment in which they can be successful and that most resembles that of their peers.

Public School Special Education staff: The umbrella of Special Education staff, funded by special education moneys and mandated by Special Education law include paraprofessionals, specially credentialed teachers, trained and credentialed specialists in the areas of speech and language, deaf and hard of hearing, vision impairments, adaptive physical education, occupational therapists, school and clinical psychologists, inclusion specialists, and other consultants.

Resource Specialist: A Special Education teacher who does not usually have his or her own classroom, and generally serves children in pull-out sessions or within their general education classroom. The RSP is also in charge of supervising the accommodations and modifications for a child as written in the IEP. RSP's generally have a caseload of up to 30 students and as well as direct teaching, are in charge of all the paperwork and meetings for these children. They also do academic assessment for children who are referred by the general education staff, and provide consultation for the general education teachers at his or her school site.

Severe Emotional Disabilities: Some children are eligible for Special Education services because of emotional and behavioral problems that keep them from functioning successfully within their classrooms or in social interactions. They may be organic in nature or caused by trauma, neglect, or injury. In the most extreme situations, these children may be placed in a special school placement where their challenging needs can be best addressed

Special Day Class: A Special Day Class (SDC) is a separate classroom for children with diagnosed and significant special needs who have not been successful academically or socially within a general education classroom. These classes have smaller class size than general education classes, and are taught by a trained Special Education teacher. The Special Day Class teacher is in charge of all meetings and paperwork for his or her students.

Special Education: This is a broad term that in public schools refers to students with diagnosed disabling conditions meeting eligibility requirements in the state education code, as well as the staff who are specially trained and credentialed to work with these students. The term also includes the structure and legal mandates that govern federally and state funded programs. My career coincidentally began at the same time as some of the major federal laws for rights for the "handicapped" were birthed. Public Law 94–142, forever imprinted in my memory, mandated that public schools provide necessary Special Education services for eligible individuals from ages three to twenty-one.

Special Education Local Plan Area: Several school districts within a geographic area that work together to support and offer joint services and classes that a single district would not be able to afford alone.

Honors & Gratitude

There were times in my working life when I felt strongly independent (or very lonely, depending upon the day) but teamwork matters. This list spotlights a few. To…

Kathy, Helen and Nita, Joan, Jane, and my other early Camelot colleagues, thank you, and of course Neva, Tom, Leslye, Margaret - you molded more than my working life. I must thank Vanta, Sally, Patty, Gayle, Judi, Susan, Sue, and Val for their constant assistance and quiet capabilities.

Dear friend Patti with your sautéing garlic, and hundreds of other awesome General Education teacher friends, you taught me more than any university class. And three cheers for visionary principals like Bill and June. My team - Theresa, Sue, Marissa, Barbara, Kate, Kelly, and Judy, you're the best!

Memory is a strange friend, and I know I will forget to thank someone important. I am profoundly sorry for omissions. Believe me, my heart knows you were there by my side when I needed you. So let me just add my gratitude for...

General Education teachers, Principals, Directors, Special Education colleagues, a multitude of gifted Specialists and faithful Volunteers, and a big thanks to my helpful Custodians over the years.

The uncountable throngs of children I taught all those thirty-eight years, who individually connected with me and changed me. Your faces fill my soul, and you are forever children in my memory. A thank you to all your parents for trusting me to be your teacher. A special thanks to my students Gregory, Jordan, two remarkable Jessicas, John, Zachary, and Kira for allowing me to share your photos, notes, poems and drawings in this memoir.

Thank you Cynthia Leslie-Boles, my writing coach, who took a raw piece of new writing and in January of 2013 gave it hope to be a presentable memoir, and to Jinx McCombs and Judy Vargas for faithful copy editing. Enormous thanks to Dinah Sanders and Joe Gratz for their design efforts.

Hugs to the over fifty friends and family members who read this memoir in its more personal and unpolished stage, full of real names and places. Every one of you helped mold this memoir.

To my husband David, my gratitude never stops flowing for your ever-giving spirit.

My extended family and upbringing gave me the underlying sensibility and sensitivity to gradually learn the lessons that my life's work laid out for me.

And love to my sons, Jackson and Alexander. I gave you my

heart and you gave me yours back three decades now. As the sons of two teachers, you have walked this path with me, and I am so thankful for the treasure of your company. I hope you still consider yourselves Teachers' Kids.

And finally to our talented Shannon, best wishes in your well-suited new career in Special Education. You already live out many of these lessons.

Postscript

It is 2015 now. As I reread this memoir in preparation for publishing, I have a nib of a worry. I wonder if anyone reading this book will feel that Mrs. B comes across as all patient, wise, and compassionate. As anyone who knows me will vehemently verify...there is no Saint C'Anna!

Every word I wrote in this memoir is authentic, but perhaps I didn't mention enough the days of self-doubt, the times I was so steamed at Someone or The System that I almost burst, the moments I ranted and raved, and complained and, yes, cursed. All of these behaviors were liberally sprinkled like salt and pepper into the big soup pot of my thirty-eight years of teaching.

So why didn't I dwell on those ranting and raving moments? This is why. In the end what stayed the course for me were the human encounters. When I sat down to write, I remembered the hard work, the mistakes made and the life lessons learned, the love given, and the satisfaction I received. What remained with me was the grace of the whole nine yards of my teaching career.

For colleagues in the teaching field, you who are just starting out and others with years of experience, this grace is what I hope you are ready to give and receive. In my opinion, this is the most important "stuff" of education and life.

And if there is anyone reading this book who is not working in education, I hope you will also understand that these lessons are much bigger than simply for special educators. The flag I am waving is that the lessons my work taught me are universal.

Warmly,
mrs. B

49434941R00099

Made in the USA
Lexington, KY
07 February 2016